Ex Líbris

A. DALE CRAIN
714-309-7366

B212 © APCo

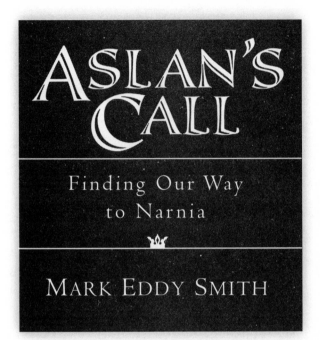

ASLAN'S CALL

Finding Our Way to Narnia

MARK EDDY SMITH

InterVarsity Press
Downers Grove, Illinois

InterVarsity Press
P.O. Box 1400, Downers Grove, IL 60515-1426
World Wide Web: www.ivpress.com
E-mail: mail@ivpress.com

InterVarsity Press® is the book-publishing division of InterVarsity Christian Fellowship/USA®, a student
movement active on campus at hundreds of universities, colleges and schools of nursing in the United States of
America, and a member movement of the International Fellowship of Evangelical Students. For information
about local and regional activities, write Public Relations Dept., InterVarsity Christian Fellowship/USA,
6400 Schroeder Rd., P.O. Box 7895, Madison, WI 53707-7895, or visit the IVCF website at
<www.intervarsity.org>.

Scripture quotations, unless otherwise noted, are from the New Revised Standard Version of the Bible,
copyright 1989 by the Division of Christian Education of the National Council of the Churches of Christ in the
USA. Used by permission. All rights reserved.

Reflection and discussion questions written by Ruth Goring.

Design: Cindy Kiple
Images: Jack Stockman
ISBN 0-8308-3242-4
Printed in the United States of America ∞

Library of Congress Cataloging-in-Publication Data

Smith, Mark Eddy, 1967-
  Aslan's call: finding our way to Narnia / Mark Eddy Smith.
       p. cm.
  ISBN 0-8308-3242-4 (pbk.: alk. paper)
  1. Lewis, C. S. (Clive Staples), 1898-1963. Chronicles of Narnia. 2.
    Children's stories, English—History and criticism. 3. Christian
  fiction, English—History and criticism. 4. Fantasy fiction,
  English—History and criticism. 5. Spiritual life in literature. 6.
  Narnia (Imaginary place) 7. God in literature. I. Title
  PR6023.E926C5395 2005
  823'.914—dc22

                                                                    2004029840

| P | 15 | 14 | 13 | 12 | 11 | 10 | 9 | 8 | 7 | 6 | 5 | 4 | 3 | 2 | 1 |
| Y | 15 | 14 | 13 | 12 | 11 | 10 | 09 | 08 | 07 | 06 | 05 | | | | | |

Contents

Abbreviations ❧ 7

Introduction ❧ 9

The Lion, the Witch and the Wardrobe ❧ 15

Prince Caspian ❧ 29

The Voyage of the *Dawn Treader* ❧ 39

The Silver Chair ❧ 51

The Horse and His Boy ❧ 65

The Magician's Nephew ❧ 73

The Last Battle ❧ 85

Afterword ❧ 95

Reflection and Discussion Questions ❧ 121

Editions Used ❧ 128

Abbreviations

HHB	*The Horse and His Boy*
LB	*The Last Battle*
LWW	*The Lion, the Witch and the Wardrobe*
MN	*The Magician's Nephew*
PC	*Prince Caspian*
SC	*The Silver Chair*
VDT	*The Voyage of the "Dawn Treader"*

Introduction

I am told there is a lion who wants to meet with me. I am told that he is fierce and unpredictable and very large. I have known about him for most of my life, and at times I've believed I caught a glimpse of his shadow, but I have yet to actually meet him face to face. His name is Aslan, and it's possible that you've heard of him.

My impression of this lion was different when I was a boy; he was simpler and, well, smaller. I mean, I realized that he wasn't entirely a lion, or at least, not only a lion. At least once he was clearly a lamb. Who cooked fish. I understood that Aslan was the son of the Emperor-over-the-sea, that he created Narnia and that he wasn't entirely constrained to Narnia, but what I failed to notice when I was a boy were the hints, at times almost blatant, that Aslan might be, well, Jesus. Of Nazareth.

Let me hasten to add that I realize Aslan is only make-believe. A lot of people wonder if I can tell the difference between fantasy and reality, but I know as well as you do that lions can't talk, beavers can't sew, and falling stars are really just chunks of space debris that burn up in our atmosphere, as opposed to, you know, actual stars. I know that Narnia is a place that Clive Staples Lewis made up back in the mid-nineteen hundreds, while Nazareth is real and so is Jesus.

I also know that where knowledge fails, belief can triumph, and I've learned, in part from a chapter in *Mere Christianity* called "Let's Pretend," that when belief falters, make-believe can sometimes take its place. For the purposes of this book I will endeavor to make believe that Narnia is real, that Aslan has landed and that I am not too old to take part in the adventure.

I had hoped when I was boy never to lose the child in me, but life has inflicted its pound (or so) of flesh, and I am older at heart than I ever planned to be. I have only been here a short time compared with, say, the age of stars, but I have nonetheless been struck by the lack of real magic in this world. *Real* magic: like horses sprouting wings, boys turning into dragons or a man crossing a sea on foot.

Jesus said, "Truly I tell you, unless you change and become like children, you will never enter the kingdom of heaven" (Matthew 18:3). The specific childhood virtue to which he alluded is humility, but it cannot have escaped his attention that the thing for which children are best known is their ability to pretend, to make believe that they are mothers or fathers, Davids or Goliaths, camels or coyotes. When someone tells them there's a man who can walk on water, their eyes go wide and they gasp in astonishment, just as if they had seen it themselves. The next time they're at the beach, they give it a try, and their disappointment when they sink is profound.

Such disappointments, when they are many (and which surely include numerous inspections of coat closets, checking for snow-covered trees), lead many of us out of childhood and into the more practical matters of adulthood. We focus on our education, on providing food, shelter and security for ourselves and our dependents. We worry about the economy, distant wars, local injustice, genocide and terrorism, but feel powerless to effect any real or lasting change. The stories in the Bible tell us we can change the world, indeed that we must, and maybe we long to believe them, but it's hard because of the sinking we did when we were children.

C. S. Lewis knew this. He spent a short time in the frontline trenches during World War I until he was wounded by shrapnel. He lost good friends in the war, including one whose mother he cared for until she died in 1951. He was a lecturer and tutor at Oxford, and he hosted children evacuated from London because of World War II. He wrote the Chronicles of Narnia to entertain these children.

He began with a wardrobe and an image he had cherished in his imagination since he was sixteen, of a faun standing in the snow holding parcels. It was not till he was some way into writing *The Lion, the Witch and the Wardrobe* that Aslan came bounding in. I don't know how long it took Lewis to ascertain the lion's true identity, but while it may seem strikingly audacious for any author to introduce the God of all creation as a character in a children's story, I like to make believe that it was the Lion of Judah himself who leaped into these stories of his own volition and for his own purposes, and that Lewis was wise enough to stand back and let him in.

By saying this I am not exactly pretending that the Chronicles of Narnia are the inspired Word of God, nor that we can put our faith in Aslan when our faith in Jesus falters. That such things are possible demonstrates that make-believe can be a dangerous game. All I know is that the words and actions of Aslan have a curious effect on me, almost as if he were speaking directly to me words of comfort, acceptance and challenge. When Lucy gains new strength by burying her face in Aslan's mane and he says, "Now you are a lioness" (*PC*, chap. 10),[1] the same sensation thrills through my body that I associate with the Spirit of God.

It bends the mind a bit to imagine that after condescending to be a creature within his own creation, Jesus would further condescend to become a lion in Lewis's creation. But Jesus told Nicodemus that there was a way to be born again from above and that the Spirit, like the wind, blows where it will, so it does not seem impossible. Indeed, it would reveal something profound about God if it could be shown to be true. But that would be a job for an adult theologian, while I am merely suggesting it with the temerity of a child.

Imagine if God were the type of Person who would enjoy

---

[1]Because the Chronicles have been published in a variety of editions over the years, here and elsewhere I refer to chapter number rather than page. The specific editions from which I quote are listed at the back of this book.

dressing up like a Lion to participate in a story for children. It would be as if a child asked the president of the United States to play hide-and-seek in the Rose Garden, and the president left the company of politicians, reporters, heads of state and the like and did just that. Lewis concludes his "Let's Pretend" chapter by writing,

> In a sense you might even say it is God who does the pretending. The Three-Personal God, so to speak, sees before Him in fact a self-centred, greedy, grumbling, rebellious human animal. But He says, "Let us pretend that this is not a mere creature, but our Son. It is like Christ in so far as it is a Man, for He became Man. Let us pretend that it is also like Him in Spirit. Let us treat it as if it were what in fact it is not. Let us pretend in order to make the pretence into a reality." God looks at you as if you were a little Christ: Christ stands beside you to turn you into one. I daresay this idea of a divine make-believe sounds rather strange at first. But, is it so strange really? Is not that how the higher thing always raises the lower? A mother teaches her baby to talk by talking to it as if it understood long before it really does. We treat our dogs as if they were "almost human": that is why they really become "almost human" in the end.

When I was growing up in New Hampshire, my next-door neighbors, Marion and Margaret, had a dog named Jason, a big black Labrador retriever with eerily empty eyes. One day my family and I were visiting with them in their living room. Jason, no doubt craving attention, stared intently at the group of us sitting on the couch. Suddenly, in the midst of our conversation, he started talking. In a voice pitched to the volume of our voices and with a declarative inflection, he said, "Ruh-ruh-ruh-ruh-ruh."

I suspect most people familiar with dogs have similar stories. The point is, make-believe almost works even with dogs. As God applies it to us, we may never get much beyond a divine equivalent of "Ruh-ruh-ruh-ruh-ruh," but I believe God will respond to our attempt with the delight of a child. ✤

The Lion, the Witch and the Wardrobe

I t's hard to imagine anything more depressing than a place that is "always winter and never Christmas," and yet the reality, when we first encounter Narnia, is hauntingly beautiful. Lucy, searching for the wardrobe's back, finds the coats giving way to branches, snow crunching beneath her feet. In a moment she reaches a pool of light cast by a solitary lamppost in the middle of a dark wood, and the snow is falling through the light with a patter that accentuates the silence. Can you hear it? Can you feel the snowflakes falling on your hair? Can you smell the cold pine trees?

The beauty of Narnia cannot be quenched by an evil spell. Winter may be a symbol of death and bereavement, but snowflakes are exquisitely beautiful. Even the loneliness and longing that are inherent to winter have a depth and poignancy that cannot be extinguished. Lucy does not enter a land that is desolate but one that overflows with wonder and magic, even from within its icy shackles. This is what makes Narnia worth saving; this is what makes Narnia similar to Earth.

When Tumnus the faun emerges into the light, holding an umbrella over his packages and his tail over his arm, the wonder and magic crystallize into a form that is capable of inviting Lucy home to tea.

WHAT CHILDREN BRING TO NARNIA

Tumnus is also capable of betraying Lucy to the Witch. He changes his mind about that because Lucy is charming, sweet-tempered and innocent, characteristics that evoke his own essential character. In a big world it can be difficult to imagine how someone as small as ourselves can make a difference. If you're like me, you can imagine grand schemes wherein you single-handedly end a war, or bring food to hungry people, or invent some way to produce clean water in arid regions, but Lucy wins the victory of Tumnus's heart simply by being herself. It's a job for which she is uniquely qualified, and though she's not yet aware of any larger purpose, its success is vital to the cancellation of winter.

But what if you, like me, are not so good and sweet as Lucy?

Edmund also has a vital role to play, but he is mean and selfish and takes little pleasure in being a child. Thus he is the perfect candidate for coming face to face with the Witch. She, as Tumnus did with Lucy, sees some of herself in Edmund, specifically his greed and pride, and this fills her with confidence that the Pevensies pose no great threat to her control. It is hardly a glorious mission, but he succeeds in it, and the Witch's winter is one step closer to its end.

Each of the children brings a necessary virtue into Narnia, which is reflected in their response to hearing the name Aslan for the first time. Peter brings the same adventuresome spirit and gift of leadership that inspired the others to join him in exploring the house the first day it rained. At the name of Aslan, he "felt suddenly brave and adventurous." Lucy brings her receptiveness and sense of wonder. Aslan's name for her invokes the feeling of freedom that comes at the end of term. Susan brings her practical common sense. Lewis elsewhere seems to frown on people who are "practical," but without Susan the four of them might not have thought to put on fur coats when first they entered Lantern Waste, and without those coats the children would have suffered throughout the first leg of their adventure. She may have a tendency toward bossiness and a desire to seem more grown up then she actually is, but the name of Aslan fills her with the same sensation one gets from some delicious smell or "delightful strain of music" (*LWW*, chap. 7). Peter and Lucy, the eldest and the youngest, are far more virtuous than the two middle children, but their virtues are rooted in a steadfastness of character. Susan and Edmund are more mixed in their composition. They are not ideals held up as examples for us to emulate; rather, they give us hope that we too, for all our impurities of soul and desire, may have some part to play in a world like Narnia.

For Aslan does not call us to be anyone other than ourselves.

Edmund's deficiencies cause Narnia to be a hellish place for him, and Aslan's name produces in him "a sensation of mysterious horror" (*LWW*, chap. 7), both because he is incapable of properly appreciating the wonder and beauty of Narnia and because the things he does appreciate, namely Turkish Delight and the promise of power, lead him inexorably to become enslaved to the Witch. While his brother and sisters are receiving gifts from Father Christmas and enjoying the miraculous return of spring, Edmund is enduring a forced march at the end of a whip. Because of the choices he has freely made out of the crookedness of his heart, he has become one more prisoner of the Witch, wretched and in need of rescue.

Fortunately for Edmund, one of Aslan's primary characteristics is his desire and determination to rescue those whom he loves.

WHAT ASLAN CAN BRING TO CHILDREN

What would it be like to meet Aslan face to face? It's a question I'm not sure I can answer, so I watch very closely when the Pevensies hear Aslan's name for the very first time.

If their first responses to hearing his name are rooted in their identity, then why do their identities seem to evaporate the first time they catch sight of him? Peter, the eldest, the leader, the adventurous one, balks and asks Mr. Beaver to go before them. When Mr. Beaver demurs, the future High King, in a mockery of chivalry, turns to Susan and says, "Ladies first." Susan, for her part, though she often wishes to seem older than she is, retorts, "No, you're the eldest." At last Peter pulls himself together, draws his sword and moves forward. "Come on," he says. "Pull yourselves together" (*LWW,* chap. 12).

Although this is a fairly amusing scene, it highlights my main worry: that I will lose my identity, my self, in the presence, full and awesome, of Aslan. Jesus says, on more than one occasion, "Those who want to save their life will lose it, and those who lose their life for my sake will find it."[2] I've always taken these verses more or less literally (that is, as losing life, as dying), and indeed Aslan could kill me. If I understood the horror of the sins I've committed, I'd probably believe that he should. If he doesn't kill me, however, if he chooses not to, then he owns me. Since he has spared my life, my life belongs to him. But I don't want to give it to him. I want to keep it.

As I continue to watch him with the Pevensies, I see him name each one, and behold! their identities are returned, and nothing is required. They stand in his presence and are not consumed, and the silence is not awkward. I'm almost ready to approach him myself, but now he's sending the girls off to be ministered to while he walks Peter over to catch a glimpse of the castle in which he's to be High King. Wow. This Aslan is all right. But wait, is that Susan's horn I hear?

All the good creatures of Narnia are ready to rush to Susan's aid, but Aslan calls them off. "Back! Let the Prince win his spurs!" And Peter is running, sword in hand and heart in throat, to attack the wolf that is snapping at his sister's heels, and it's like

---

[2]Matthew 16:25; Mark 8:35; similarly Matthew 10:39; Luke 9:24-25; 17:33; John 12:25.

a nightmare with the teeth and the blood and the heavy, gamey-smelling fur sliding all over him, and what happened to the magical world of talking animals and sudden springs?

Somehow or other the wolf ends up dead, and Susan is climbing down from the tree and there's hugging and kissing, and really, for his first battle Peter didn't do too badly. He turns to Aslan with the beginnings of a shaky grin, and Aslan—Aslan criticizes him for forgetting to clean his sword.

This has always bothered me. Assuming that Peter, a London lad from the year 1940, has never had formal training in swordsmanship (though presumably he has read enough of the right kinds of books to understand the rules of chivalry), it would seem to me that he has just accomplished a tremendous feat and should be praised for it. Instead he is shamed for letting five minutes pass between killing a gigantic wolf and wiping the wolf's insides off his sword.

Upon closer reading, I have to concede that there is no evidence that Aslan intends to make Peter feel ashamed, and indeed he promptly knights the boy on the field of battle, dubbing him Sir Peter Wolfs-Bane. This is praise enough, but Peter nonetheless blushes and is obviously embarrassed by his lapse, and I expect Aslan to be more, well, sensitive. But it occurs to me that perhaps Aslan is rebuking Peter gruffly because he wants Peter to see brave acts such as this as things a High King should do as a matter of course, with no expectation of praise.

Also, if I think about it from a different perspective, Aslan probably really loved that big bad wolf. He had known the creature from puphood, and no doubt had had higher hopes for him.

ASLAN'S HUMILITY

No one ever hears what Aslan and Edmund talk about as they walk together apart from the rest of the court the morning after his rescue, but "it was a conversation which Edmund never forgot" (*LWW,* chap. 13), and he comes away from it greatly changed. One imagines that the Witch did a lot of the prep work for his reformation, for as the Bible tells us, "suffering . . . produces character" (Romans 5:3-4). The Witch's treatment of Edmund and her intentions for the other Pevensie children were meant for evil, but Aslan uses them for good. Edmund's choices, his complicity with the Witch, make him heinously guilty, yet after speaking with the lion for a while he is content to do nothing but stand and stare at Aslan while the Witch presents her accusation against him.

Similarly, Aslan's conversation with the Witch is off the record. When he calls his followers back, all he tells them is that the Witch has relinquished her claim on Edmund. He tells no one of the deal he has made with her.

This is different from the time he did much the same thing on Earth. One difference is that his sacrifice in Narnia is not for everyone, for Narnia is not a place where everyone needs to be redeemed. On Earth, Jesus told his disciples that he would be handed over to death but would afterward return. Not that anyone knew what he meant.

Aslan is supremely powerful and yet profoundly humble. Seeing what Aslan conceals makes me wonder what stories about Jesus are missing from the Gospels. Some of the best parts of his incredible story may have occurred without witness, or at least without literate witnesses. Even what we know may have succumbed to the problem faced by all writers throughout history: that it is impossible to convey in words the essence of the very best stories.

The only reason anyone knows what happens later that night is that Susan and Lucy cannot sleep. What a touching reversal of the Gospel story of the disciples who could "not stay awake . . . one hour" (Matthew 26:40). The two girls wander into the night to search for Aslan, and when they find him he condescends to let them walk with him awhile, because he is "sad and lonely" (*LWW,* chap. 14).

Whoa. I have always heard the anguish in Jesus' voice when he prayed in Gethsemane, and I have always felt a stab of guilt when he admonishes the disciples for not being able to stay awake (since I can so readily identify with them), but never until I really considered this scene in Narnia did I come to understand the simple, awful truth about Gethsemane: Jesus was sad and lonely.

Think about it. The history of the world hung in the balance that night. I'm not talking about religion here, I'm not trying to get you to believe if you don't already, I'm just trying to put myself in that garden, with Jesus, two thousand years ago. I turned thirty-three a few years ago. I'm not ready to die yet. But everything Jesus did was directed toward his crucifixion, and when it came right down to it, he was terrified. My God, so would I be.

There's only so much preparation you can do for something like that. Tomorrow you will die. If you want to, you can call on legions of your father's angels to turn away the moment, and truth to tell, your Father will understand. The world is full of violence and evil, and there have been plenty of times when he's wanted to destroy the whole thing anyway. The only reason to keep going is if you love your friends enough to save them from themselves. And this night they're not even helping. They're falling asleep while the whole earth teeters on the brink. You don't have to do this. But there's John to think about, and James, even Peter, who will deny you later tonight: Are they worth saving? Do they mean that much to you?

This is the value of Aslan to me: that I can empathize with him as he offers up himself in exchange for Edmund, and through him, I can understand Jesus in a whole new way. It's so much easier to come at it through the lens of fiction. Wow, Aslan would do that for one bratty little kid, because he loves him. With awe, something approaching true awe, I turn that understanding toward the nonfictional account of Jesus of Nazareth, a guy from the Middle East who lived a long time ago, whom I've never physically met, who was nailed to a crossbeam and lifted onto a post, wrists and feet nailed, nails pounded through flesh into wood. Ow. And left there. To die. His mom before him crying. A couple of friends. The sky goes dark, as if it knows how you feel, and yes, it's easier in a way than the night before, because now you don't have so much of a choice. You've come this far, you might as well see it through. But then there's the dying, the inability to breathe, the dripping blood from the crown of thorns, blood dripping slowly down your face and no way to wipe it away, because your hands . . .

How many times can we think about this? How long can this image retain its power? It's been two *thousand* years. Other people have died in similarly horrible ways. But this was done for you. This was done for me. One of the most difficult things we have to accept in this culture of human rights and recourse to the law, excellent things both, is that we who are for the most part law-abiding citizens deserve this, deserve anything like this. Surely there's nothing we've ever done to deserve death, let alone a painful one. We should ease suffering wherever and whenever possible. . . .

But Edmund, I can relate to Edmund. I have betrayed, I have fallen woefully short of everything I was meant to be. I understand why Edmund deserved to die for the sin he tried to commit. Well, I think I do. All right, maybe I don't, but I understand that it's written on the Emperor's scepter, and why it is, and so why the Enemy has claim through that law to Edmund's life. And I understand Aslan's motivation for wanting to save Edmund, because he spoke with him, and he's not such a bad kid really, just the third child of four, feeling neglected, wanting attention, doesn't know how to get it except by being bratty, but he has potential, anyone can see that. If someone would just forgive him this once, give him a second chance, let him know that his life has value—oh, the things he could do, the friends he could befriend, the encouragement he could give to others.

It helps, you know, that there's a magic deeper still. That you know ahead of time that death is not the end. But this knowledge doesn't really help the dying, even if, as Narnia makes it seem, the son of the Emperor-over-the-sea does this on a fairly regular basis. There's still the joy of life and the sorrow and terror of death, the submission to that which is evil for the sake of that which is not wholly evil yet. That which may yet be saved.

"I am sad and lonely." How can a fictional talking lion convey so well the admixture of human, utterly human, and profoundly divine nature of Jesus long after the biblical account has come to seem like something you read at the Easter Vigil and maybe it gives you the shivers and maybe it doesn't? At least in Narnia he is not wholly alone.

ESSENTIAL SACRIFICE

Aslan begins the war against the Witch by offering his life and follows through by submitting to death. Of course it is not enough for her. She doesn't want the death of one; she wants control of everyone and everything at all times forever. That's what separates Aslan from the Witch and God from Satan. God is all about relinquishing power, because power is not his ultimate goal. He wants to live in peace with his friends. So Aslan does not put up a fight, nor even offer any grand speeches to those who would bind and kill him. He lets them have their way with him, and then he dies.

So great is Aslan's humility that he protects the innocence of his creatures even from the horror of seeing him dead. Ordinary field mice in the hundreds gnaw through the cords that bind his corpse. No other creatures in Narnia could have performed that service so gently or efficiently. Susan, by nature of her personality, is horrified, and Lucy, of course, is more perceptive. Aslan is free, and his resurrection is one more off-stage event. His mane is restored, and if he was sad and lonely before, he is now overflowing with joy. He explains about the Deeper Magic to the girls and says, "And now—"

And Lucy says, "Oh yes. Now?" (*LWW,* chap. 15).

Then, though the battle is already engaged, though there are statues to unstone and evil to defeat, the time has come for a rollicking game of tag. Whether their playmate more resembles a thunderstorm or a kitten the girls can't tell, but they understand that the time has come to celebrate, because whatever battles may be left to fight, the war is over. Joy must be spent frivolously or not at all, because without joy there can be no victory. Joy is the victory.

Of course it can't be repeated enough: Aslan is not a safe playmate. When he roars, stop your ears. When he lets you ride on his back, hold on tight. When he breathes on the feet of a stone giant, well, tell yourself he knows what he's doing and hope for the best. And when the giant asks for a handkerchief, offer yours, and be grateful that two handkerchiefs are all you lose in Narnia.

Finally, when tending to your wounded brother, remember that though his life was purchased at great price, it is no more valuable than the lives of others. When Lucy applies her cordial to his wound and wants to wait for it to take effect before moving on to other wounded, Aslan asks, "Must *more* people die for Edmund?" Her response is simple and utterly appropriate: "I'm sorry, Aslan," she says and immediately gets up to tend to the others. When she returns, Edmund "had become his real old self again and could look you in the face" (*LWW,* chap. 17). The wound that Lucy was so anxious about proves to be the least of the healing Edmund has undergone, and yes, by now I believe Aslan is someone I can trust with my life and my identity.

When they process to Cair Paravel, the narrator asks a tantalizing question. Describing the castle and the sea, and the sound of the gulls, he writes, "Have you heard it? Can you remember?" (*LWW,* chap. 17). Whether due to the fact that I've been reading these books since childhood or for some other reason, I half-fancy I do remember.

Later, when they have become Kings and Queens and grown-ups, they embark on a quest. The white stag has been sighted, who grants wishes if you can catch it. The danger of pursuing such a quarry is that if you *don't* catch it you run the risk of losing the wish that's already been granted. Susan alone balks from following the stag past the lamppost, though they all intuit that their fortunes will change drastically if they do. I think it's possible that Susan never gets over her disappointment at returning to Earth, where she isn't a queen, where her clothes, however stylish, will never quite measure up. But I will have more to say about Susan later on. ❧

27

Prince Caspian

More than any other Chronicle, *Prince Caspian* is a story about the power of stories. Stories are not perhaps the most objective source when one seeks evidence that stories are vital to life, faith and action (except insofar as such things are self-evident), but the stories-within-stories format of *Prince Caspian* nicely illustrates the fact that one simply cannot act without constructing some sort of story to provide context and meaning for one's life.

In *The Lion, the Witch and the Wardrobe,* the Witch tells Edmund a story that features him usurping Peter's place as High King. He accepts the story and acts accordingly, betraying his siblings. Aslan has a different story, one in which Edmund and Peter take their rightful places as King and High King respectively. Aslan is willing to do most anything to make sure that his story comes true, and he requires Edmund's willing participation, which is something else that separates Aslan's story from the Witch's. Stories are pervasive, and the ability to live well in this world or any other is contingent on choosing Aslan's story over the Witch's and being able to tell the difference.

THE POWER AND THE PERIL OF STORIES

Sitting at a train station on their way back to school, the Pevensies are magically pulled into a thicket. Once they push themselves out of the clinging and poking branches, they find themselves on a beach. "Five minutes later everyone was barefooted and wading in the cool clear water" (*PC*, chap. 1). The children assume that the story they've landed in is basically an extension of their summer holidays. In any event, they would rather play in the ocean than waste time wrestling with existential questions like "Where are we?" and "Why are we here?" I can't say I fault them for it, but when they're sitting in the ruins of what any fool can see is plainly Cair Paravel a thousand years in the future, they have to reason out every detail of their likely location like a shipwrecked Socrates. It's a sad fact of life that stories are always murkier and more convoluted when we're in the midst of them than when we're reading them.

The fact that the Pevensies arrive in Cair Paravel instead of Aslan's How, where Caspian and his army really need them, is as puzzling as any aspect of a true story. But the reasons are straightforward. Just imagine if they had landed in the midst of a pitched battle! They need to acclimate themselves and retrieve the presents Father Christmas gave them in *The Lion, the Witch and the Wardrobe*. They also need to rescue Trumpkin from drowning and to hear the story behind the battle they are about to engage in.

Wonderfully, the only reason Trumpkin wastes his time telling the story is that he has no faith in it. He wasn't expecting anyone to show up in answer to the horn, and even when he's proved wrong, he refuses to believe that the children will be of any help. For all the wrong reasons, then, he takes the time to tell the whole story of Caspian, when otherwise he might have thought it more important to rush them into battle unprepared.

Miraz, in contrast, understands the power of stories, as everyone in a position of power must. The only problem is that his stories are lies. In his stories he is the rightful king, the woods are haunted, and there was never any such thing as animals who could talk. So powerful are these stories that he almost believes them himself. When Caspian was young, Miraz endeavored to keep him ignorant of true or even fanciful stories, knowing they were liable to make him strong-willed and mindful of such things as freedom and justice, not to mention truth. Nevertheless, first Caspian's nurse and then his tutor told him true stories of Old Narnia, fairy tales of talking animals, glorious adventures and a lion.

The reason people like Caspian's nurse and tutor have some hope of escaping Miraz's notice is that, paradoxically, the tyrant's familiarity with lies leaves him particularly vulnerable to being duped. He has no framework for understanding the source of true stories. He never suspects Caspian's nurse, for he can plainly see she has no power of her own, at least not what he would consider power, till he discovers that his young nephew has no other desire than to live the fairy tales she's taught him. That he would turn around and immediately hire a half-dwarf for the job of tutor is no more surprising: he has come under the power of his own stories and no longer believes in Old Narnia. He assumes that attention to a practical education will bring Caspian under that same power. He could not be more wrong.

THE TOUCH OF WONDER

There is something in a child that bursts open at the touch of wonder, and it is difficult, though not impossible, to unburst it shut. Stories can evoke that wonder, can prime the pump as it were, but they never bring the touch of wonder, only an approximation. The true stories Caspian hears produce a yearning for wonder, so that he tries to talk to his cats, but it is not until Cornelius brings him out onto the tower for a lesson in astronomy that real wonder reaches down and tousles his hair.

Stargazing is slow and crickenating work. Doubtless the stars in Narnia, being younger, brighter and closer than those seen from Earth, dance to a somewhat quicker drum, but even so, the waltzes they weave require concentration and an extraordinarily long attention span. Nevertheless, there is something about them that commands one's attention. It's as if they go slowly in order that those who watch may understand. Perhaps it is this enhanced concentration that allows Caspian to grasp the obvious truth about his tutor.

When he finally sees the proof of the stories in the Doctor's face, when he finally understands that before him stands a real-life dwarf (half-dwarf notwithstanding), Caspian finds himself caught between joy and terror. On the one hand he fears the Doctor will kill him out of a heretofore hidden hatred that will be revealed alongside his surprising identity. On the other hand is wonder, the joy sparked by the epiphany, the sudden understanding that all the old stories are true and Old Narnia is still alive. The latter overpowers the former, so that his fear becomes a little thing. Is death of any consequence in the face of such joy? It is to Caspian's credit that he recognizes this, that he yields to the joy where his uncle and others of his uncle's generation would choose instead to submit to terror.

When the day comes that the birth of Miraz's son endangers Caspian's life, he is sent out into the world armed primarily with his understanding of the stories his nurse and tutor told him. By some miracle it is sufficient.

NOT PEACE BUT A SWORD

After the forces of nature unhorse him and lay him flat, Caspian is taken in by two full-blooded dwarfs and a Talking Badger. Apparently they have been living together in relative harmony up until Caspian arrives and brings the differences between them into stark relief. Trufflehunter says, "I'm a beast, I am, and a Badger what's more. We don't change. We hold on" (*PC*, chap. 5). He understands Caspian's significance as a true King of Narnia and welcomes his arrival. But dwarfs are perhaps a little too much like humans: Nikabrik believes that the only way to get out from under someone's thumb is to cut off the thumb. He wants nothing more than to kill Caspian, both because of who he is and because of what he represents. Trumpkin is more moderate than either of his housemates: he has no more use for fairy tales than Miraz, but he will on no account consent to the murder of a guest.

In a society where nothing much is happening, even when the status quo is not so good, it's relatively easy to be tolerant. But when action comes a-knocking, people argue. Sometimes it's about a big thing like whether to invite ogres and hags to join the effort, and other times it's about whether to talk first and eat later, or vice versa, or to attempt both simultaneously. This may have been what Jesus meant when he said he had "not come to bring peace, but a sword" (Matthew 10:34). They decide to begin with a war council because it's hard to talk back to a centaur, but as it turns out they needn't have bothered arguing, because Doctor Cornelius crashes their party and informs them that Miraz is on the move.

They retreat to Aslan's How, where battle ensues. It does not go well. Stories are good for many things, but they are no substitute for field experience when one needs to coordinate a battle plan, and giants, even good ones, are not known for their intelligence. So they decide to blow Susan's magical horn and argue about whom to send to meet whatever emissaries of Aslan might arrive.

The stories that Nikabrik lives by are full of anger and suspicion; he refuses to go because "there must be a Dwarf here to see that the Dwarfs are fairly treated." It's a compelling rationale because it sounds altruistic, but it breeds further anger and suspicion. Trumpkin counters, not by arguing against Nikabrik's stated motives but by volunteering to go himself. He says, "I know the difference between giving advice and taking orders" (*PC*, chap. 7). Magically, the argument is over, and Trumpkin has chosen a side.

This is Aslan's own method for resolving conflict: to take the brunt of the argument on oneself. It may cost your life, as Trumpkin finds when he is captured by the Seneschal, but Susan's arrow and the false stories of ghosts on the island forge his redemption. (Funny how false stories have a way of twisting out from under those who propagate them.) It's a simple technique, surprisingly effective and at times quite painful. It's basically a matter of grabbing hold of your opponent's sword from the wrong end.

A LIMIT TO UNDERSTANDING

I said before that stories are no substitute for experience, but what are we to make of the Pevensies as they thrash through the woods trying to reach Caspian in time? They have heard the stories, they have firsthand experience of Aslan, and yet when he shows up they can't see him and won't follow Lucy, who does. The sad fact of the matter is that not even experience and stories together are enough to combat our stubborn insistence on doing things our own way.

One gets the sense that only Lucy can see him because only she is prepared to see him, that it is not Aslan's choice to be invisible to them but their own. Lucy is never about leading or finding her own way but is always willing to follow those older and wiser (or at least more opinionated) than she. So nothing is in the way of her seeing Aslan. Edmund, at least, learned enough from his part of their previous story and was humbled enough by it, that he chooses Lucy's vision over his own. The others wait; only when their own way has led them into arrows and sent them running will they consent to follow their clear-sighted sister. Eventually their eyes begin to change, and Aslan is visible to them as well, but this may be the point in the adventure at which Peter and Susan prove themselves too old to return anymore to Narnia.

When Caspian arrives at his lowest moment, when a hag and a wer-wolf are proposing to raise the White Witch, he does not know that High King Peter and his brother King Edmund are listening at the door. But he manages nonetheless to understand, without virtue of knowledge or experience, that though help may be hideously delayed, no good will come of turning to more present help when Aslan is not available. By this Caspian proves that he is not like Saul, who as 1 Samuel 28 relates, raised the spirit of the prophet when God would not speak to him, and thereby lost his throne and his sons and in the end took his own life. What separates Caspian from Saul? The answer involves simple-sounding things like trust, humility and obedience. But as I compare the stories of Caspian and Saul, I am filled with dread, for I fear that I more resemble Saul.

Aslan, at any rate, seems to have complete trust in Caspian. While Peter, Edmund and Trumpkin are bursting in at the last possible moment to begin to save the day, he is preparing a feast with Susan and Lucy. The following day, while Peter is engaging in mortal combat with Miraz, Aslan is directing Bacchus and his wild girls to rip down the Bridge of Beruna, following which they all march into the village to frighten away everyone who isn't overjoyed to see them.

Battles are dire and bloody, and history seems to hang in the balance while they are being fought, but they are not necessarily the most important things as far as Aslan is concerned. The people in Beruna are living under the terrible oppression of routine, the same boring thing every day. The story they have been told is that work and school are the most important things in life. Aslan walks into Beruna and gives the lie to that story. "Ho, everyone who thirsts, come to the waters; and you that have no money, come, buy and eat! Come, buy wine and milk without money and without price. Why do you spend your money for that which is not bread, and your labor for that which does not satisfy? Listen carefully to me, and eat what is good, and delight yourselves in rich food" (Isaiah 55:1-2). Not many in the town follow him, but the rescue of those who do is more important than winning the war against Miraz, who is, after all, only a man.

In the end, Aslan sets up a door and offers anyone who doesn't feel they belong in Narnia the chance to return to Earth. He provides them with two good choices: live in harmony with the beasts of Narnia or go back where they came from and have a good life there. Anyone who trusts in Aslan can enjoy the most important part of any story: a happy ending. ❧

The Voyage of the "Dawn Treader"

When we first meet Reepicheep the Mouse on the field of victory in *Prince Caspian*, it's immediately obvious that he has wholeheartedly embraced all the true stories, so that he can even go toe to toe with Aslan himself in regard to his tail, which was sacrificed in battle. Aslan hates vanity, which seems to be Reepicheep's prime motive for wanting his tail replaced, and he wishes Reepicheep to accept the loss. Two things cause him to change his mind. The first is that the Chief Mouse unquestioningly believes that Aslan can accomplish the healing for him, and the second is that all the other mice are prepared to sacrifice their own tails if their leader must be bereft of his. These are, after all, descendants of the mice who gnawed away the cords that bound Aslan when he was dead. They understand that love and sacrifice go hand in hand. By his own account, Aslan is overmatched.

But what of those who are so taken in by false stories that true ones have no allure for them? Is there no hope for those who are too dull or stupid to realize even their need for rescue?

THE DRAGON WITHIN, THE DRAGON WITHOUT

Eustace has many opportunities to avoid the fate that awaits him on Dragon Isle. He is, after all, on a most marvelous adventure, he has been taught a lesson in honor by a most illustrious and noble Mouse, and he has been shown to be of almost no value in his current state, according to the scales of the slave trade. He could have followed any of these doors into a truer self-understanding and a new way of living, but he cannot see that the doors lead anywhere particularly interesting. He persists in his tiresome insistence that he is being unduly put upon by ignorant and selfish people. In other words, he sees his attempted rescuers as jailers, holding the keys from him out of spite. So when the *Dawn Treader* limps into a harbor after a devastating storm, Eustace feels fully justified in wandering away from camp to get some time to himself. For his trouble he gets exactly what he deserves: he gets to see himself as he truly is.

Imagine that the only thing that could possibly convince you of the reality of magic is being transformed into a monster. It's more common than you might think. In "The Weight of Glory," Lewis writes, "The dullest and most uninteresting person you can talk to may one day be a creature which, if you say it now, you would be strongly tempted to worship, or else a horror and a corruption such as you now meet, if at all, only in a nightmare."

Generally speaking, dragons are powerful, wealthy, clever and practical—all things that Eustace finds appealing. But when he discovers what he has turned into, his initial thoughts of revenge on those who have been (as he sees it) torturing him are quickly followed by the realization that "he would have been grateful for a kind word even from Reepicheep" (*VDT*, chap. 6). Immediately he lifts his head and weeps for sheer loneliness. One suspects it is the first time he has wept from his heart since he was an infant. Though he can't see it at the time, this is the moment at which he becomes capable of receiving help, for he finally understands what help he needs.

For the first time in his life, Eustace is in a condition that anyone else might call pitiable. Yet when he learns he can fly, he is, for the first time on this magnificent adventure, pleasantly surprised. The healing process has begun.

Now, for the first time, people would understand if he didn't feel much like helping. Now, for the first time, he is helpful whenever possible, going so far as to uproot a large tree as a mast for the *Dawn Treader*. He gets his wish—a kind word from Reepicheep—and is indeed grateful. Without his even noticing it, the healing of his dragonish heart has been accomplished.

The only thing left is to remove the skin. Aslan shows up for this part, because no one is so powerful that they can peel off all the layers of their own dead skin. And Edmund the former traitor is there afterward to welcome him into the community of the redeemed.

A MOUSE OF HONOR

Reepicheep is so much the opposite of Eustace that he too can be annoying at times. What I mean to say is that he puts me to shame, which I always find annoying. He is so noble and honorable and morally unambiguous that he gives the lie to my fond belief that it's better to give in occasionally to sin and thereby know intimately the weaknesses that others face (in order to have true compassion and lack of judgment toward them) than to hold myself to a higher standard and be a model for others to follow. I fear otherwise that I might become arrogant or high-handed. Reepicheep seems both arrogant and high-handed, and he may in fact be, but he is also stalwart and true, and his judgments are beyond reproach.

When the ship is attacked by a sea serpent, he throws himself against the scaly hide and nearly kills himself pushing before the rest of the crew even figure out what he's trying to do and rush to help him. A Mouse is no match for the task of pushing a ship out from under a serpent, no matter how big his heart or how determined he may be. None of them are, alone, but together they manage it, barely, because they have an example to follow.

There comes a time when everyone needs to put everything they have into one endeavor, and if they stint even a little the endeavor will fail, with disastrous consequences. Reepicheep is made for such times, and the crew might have been lost without him on several occasions, but at other times, when the utmost is not required, he is still willing at a moment's notice to give it. Which can be, as I mentioned, annoying.

On the island of the Dufflepuds, Reepicheep is invaluable as a barometer of what's the right thing to do. Being a Mouse of true valor and high honor, he does not hesitate to let someone else join him in being honorable and valorous. It is with his encouragement that Lucy accepts the adventure the Duffles present her with and faces the stairs the following morning.

The Power of Little Girls and Magicians

This island has always been more than a little magical to me. I couldn't say why exactly. The peace, I suppose, the orderliness that seems out of place in the middle of the unexplored ocean, the ordinariness of it. I've been enthralled by this island from the moment I stepped imaginary foot on it many years ago. I hope to visit someday, for I am as sure that it is a real place, one that could be got to, as I am that "when a chap's hungry, he likes some victuals," or that water is "powerful wet stuff" (*VDT*, chap. 10).

The staircase itself is magical: the ticking of the grandfather clock, the plush of the carpet, the way even the ticking dies away as the staircase takes a bend. The length of the hall, the angle of light through the windows, the carvings, the doors, the bearded mirror. At the end of the hall a door that can't be shut, books from floor to ceiling, in the middle a podium, and on it a book of spells.

As Lucy pages through the spells, she comes upon an incantation that will give her beauty beyond the lot of mortals. As soon as she finds herself tempted to incant it, Aslan appears on the page as a picture, growling. It's enough to steer Lucy away from succumbing to envy and pride, thereby averting war and the destruction of Narnia. But in a way his intervention sets her up for the next, some might say lesser, temptation of eavesdropping, which of course leads immediately to tears at the seeming betrayal of a trusted friend. Worse, this may be the episode that demonstrates that even Lucy can grow too old for Narnia, for surely the little girl from the previous Chronicles would never have been tempted much by either spell.

Immediately after comes a spell "for the refreshment of the spirit" (*VDT*, chap. 10), and I have to wonder: did Lewis realize he was describing his own book? He mentions in the hallway, "I don't know what the Bearded Glass was for because I am not a magician," but the story Lucy reads in the Magician's book must be very good indeed to rival the Chronicles of Narnia in providing refreshment for one's spirit. As many times as I have read them, they almost never fail to refresh me, and whenever I talk about a really good story, I mean one that reminds me of the long hallway leading to the Magician's Book.

At last she arrives at the spell for making visible that which is hidden, and immediately Aslan is walking up behind her. He has been there all along throughout their adventures, but he was hidden. The spell, which works only when read by a magician or a little girl, makes him visible, for he obeys his own rules. Lucy's face lights up, and "for a moment (but of course she didn't know it), she looked almost as beautiful as that other Lucy in the picture" (*VDT*, chap. 10). In my imagination she is even more beautiful at that moment, in part because the keenest beauties are unaware of themselves, and in part because delight is one of the most beautiful of expressions.

She asks Aslan if he will tell her the story she read in the Magician's Book, which she is already forgetting, and he tells her the most marvelous thing: "Indeed, yes, I will tell it to you for years and years." If there is one unbelievable thing I have learned from the Chronicles of Narnia that I believe more strongly than any other, it's that each of our lives is a story told by God that is part of, and no less wonderful than, the story Lucy read, the story "about a cup and a sword and a tree and a green hill" (*VDT*, chap. 10). But though I believe it, it is difficult to remember.

What We May Learn from the Dufflepuds

The relationship between the Magician named Coriakin and the Dufflepuds is a lot like the relationship many of us have with God. We, like the Duffers, love to gather together with like-minded folk and agree with one another about the truths of life, and invent amazing and ingenious time-saving devices. But when God tries to intervene to tell us what he would like us to do, we cower and cover our ears and try to imagine what horrible dementia put such a thought in our heads.

It reminds me of that story from the Bible, when God told Adam and Eve not to eat the fruit of that one tree. The serpent told them it was because God was withholding something good from them. But God knew all along that it was for their own good that they should keep away from it, since it would give them knowledge of good and evil, without which they could happily have done anything else that they pleased, ignorant as an ape (I don't mean a Talking Ape, of course) about whether what they did was right or wrong. I can't think of any examples of this sort of thing from my own life, but Lewis has put his finger on the truth of it. Hear him! No one ever put a better finger on a bigger truth than that!

MISSION ACCOMPLISHED

By the time they reach Ramandu's island, their quest is nominally finished, since they have found the remaining Lords, but though the Lords are found, they are not yet saved. In order to accomplish that the crew must sail as near to the end of the world as they can and leave one of their own behind.

From the moment Ramandu and his daughter sing the sun into the sky, the nature and quality of the adventure changes. "As Edmund said afterwards, 'Though lots of things happened on that trip which *sound* more exciting, that moment was really the most exciting'" (*VDT*, chap. 14). From this point on the voyage is no longer marked by battles and transformations and rescues and escapes but by a gradually building crescendo of awe. It sounds not near as exciting, and yet somehow it is more.

Now as they sail there's too much light, and the water is so clear Lucy can see the ship's shadow on the seabed. As soon as she understands that she's looking at the bottom of the ocean, she suddenly can make sense of the colors and shapes slipping past her. She sees a submarine forest and roads and merpeople. Of course Reepicheep *would* want to fight them when they rise up and shake their spears, but fortunately he is distracted by the first splash of seawater that gets in his mouth. He realizes it is not salt, but sweet, and that the prophecy that has haunted his entire life is at long last literally coming true. And that is more profoundly exciting than any battle.

As the seafarers drink the water, their eyes become stronger, able to withstand the brilliance of the light. They no longer eat or even sleep much. Their only other interaction with the people under the sea concerns only Lucy and involves nothing more than a glance, but in that glance a friendship is somehow forged. It is perhaps the most poignant moment in the entire book: "There does not seem to be much chance of their meeting again in that world or any other. But if ever they do they will rush together with their hands held out" (*VDT*, chap. 16). How many stories have you read in which making a friend seemed more exhilarating than finding a pool that turned things into gold?

Without the water to strengthen their senses, everyone on the *Dawn Treader* would have gone mad. As it is, Caspian nearly does. He and Lucy agree that the sensory overload is almost too much to bear, yet they don't want it to stop. As King, he feels it should be within his power to ensure that it never does. He wants to see the adventure through to its conclusion. More precisely, to the conclusion that he thinks would be the best. He wants to abandon his kingdom and his kingship and accompany Reepicheep to Aslan's country.

Aslan thinks differently, as Caspian finds out when he retires to his cabin in a rage, having insulted Reepicheep and generally behaved downright Eustaceish for the first time in this journey. Aslan's image comes to life in his cabin and tells him the worst news possible: he must leave Lucy, Edmund, Eustace and Reepicheep behind at once and return—to his future bride.

Too often the life of the spirit seems boring. We seem unable to imagine heaven except as a place where there is singing and praising and precious little else. But this image, for those of us who have it, is proof that we ourselves are too stupid, dull or insipid to fully comprehend the glory of true stories. In the intensity of the Last Sea, "the light, the silence, the tingling smell of the Silver Sea, even (in some odd way) the loneliness itself, were too exciting" (*VDT*, chap. 16). Somehow Caspian's seemingly insane desire makes sense: would it not be better to forgo the pleasures of wife and kingdom and to bask in the glory of the End of the World? But Caspian, like most of the rest of us, must wait until the appointed time when death will bring us to that place we most long for. At least when that time comes for Caspian he will be able to face it without fear, having caught a glimpse of what to expect.

The four who are to continue on get in the boat and glide along the current until they reach a wall of water. Their boat runs aground, and Lucy, Edmund and Eustace watch Reepicheep's coracle rush up the wall and over and, one hopes, into Aslan's Country at last. Like that of Enoch and Elijah, Reepicheep's faithfulness has earned him a translation straight out of the world, without the need for death's intervening. But before Reepicheep goes, though he cannot bring himself to be overly sad at the parting, he does allow Lucy her fondest wish, which is to pick him up and cuddle him. A worthy Mouse indeed.

At last, hand in hand, feeling more like children than they have since they left Aunt Alberta's back room, Eustace and Edmund and Lucy come across something so bright that it daunts even their water-strengthened eyes. As they get closer, they see that it is a lamb, and that it has cooked them breakfast. This perhaps is why Peter and Susan were so quiet after Aslan said goodbye to them before sending them back the last time. Here is Aslan, telling them as bluntly as he can that he has another name. He does not tell them the name, perhaps because too many people in this age have become confused and roll their eyes at the mere mention. "At the name of Jesus every eye shall roll"? I don't think that's how it's supposed to go, but that is all too often the way it is. By calling himself Aslan, Jesus has returned a measure of glory to his person, because anyone would be overjoyed to meet Aslan. It's the lamb we've become leery of.

When he tells the two Pevensies they are too old to return to Narnia and must begin to come close to their own world, Lucy blurts out, "It isn't Narnia, you know. . . . It's *you*. We shan't meet *you* there. And how can we live, never meeting you?" (*VDT*, chap. 16). Somehow, though I know this is all allegory and make-believe, I know exactly what she means: I too want to meet Aslan. But he tells them he is on Earth too, and all worlds have entrances into Aslan's Country, and he will always be telling them the way. I cling to that. ✺

The Silver Chair

How different Narnia seems without Lucy! Aslan is unaccountably harsh with Jill, worse than when he scolded Peter for not cleaning his sword. Even considering that she yanked Eustace off a cliff, she didn't do it on purpose. She's all alone in a strange place with a terrifying lion (she doesn't even know who he is!) who's telling her that if she doesn't drink from the stream he's guarding she will die of thirst. Indeed death, or the threat of death, plays a major role in this Chronicle. Aslan tells Jill that if she can't find her way back to her world, she must either rescue Rilian or die in the attempt. In no way does this seem better than the situation from which she just escaped at Experiment House.

GOOD TIMES MAKE FOR SOFT PEOPLE

Narnia itself is different: it is now a land at peace, free of oppression, spells and danger (or at least ignorant of such), but also a land (and there may be a connection here) where it is more difficult to find willing help. When times were grim, children from Earth had all the help they needed. Now, when the only thing really wrong is a Prince who's been missing ten years, and countless heroes who have been lost in vain pursuit of him, creatures are a little more reticent to lay down their lives in the name of honor, vengeance or rescue.

Thus when the owls fly Eustace and Jill away from the revelry and apathy of the castle, it is a true rescue, but the owls themselves are willing to go only so far. They tell the story of Prince Rilian (an invaluable gift, as we've already seen with Trumpkin's tale in *Prince Caspian*), but when they hear what Aslan has asked the children to do, they quail. Not that they don't have excellent reasons: owls and humans just wouldn't make good traveling companions.

The only type of person who can help the children is one who doesn't trust the good times to last and is always expecting the worst. Puddleglum considers himself the least dour of all the Marsh-wiggles, yet when the owls approach him with the children he immediately guesses that catastrophe has befallen Narnia. Far from being relieved when he learns that this is not the case, he looks to the next potential apocalypse, namely, the outcome of their mission. Of course he plans to join the mission, based at least partly on the thesis that a long and dangerous and anyhow hopeless journey will steady him, show him the serious side of life.

Eustace and Jill couldn't be happier. Puddleglum may not be the army Caspian would have sent to accompany them, but he is company, and that is a precious gift when no one else wants the job.

The three of them set off on the loneliest Narnian adventure since Edmund betrayed his siblings to the White Witch. There are no grand adventures or feasts with Aslan or even many stories, just endless hiking through lonely moors.

It is not terrible at first, and Jill even ventures that adventures aren't so bad, until Puddleglum rejoins that they haven't had any. But not even his eternal pessimism can dampen their spirits as much as the description given them by the Lady of the Green Kirtle of the reception they will receive at Harfang. Her words of hope and cheer work on their minds like Turkish Delight: the mere promise of sweetness is enough to make them unable to think of anything else.

THINGS CAN'T BE SEEN TILL THEY'RE KNOWN

When Lewis was a boy, the first time he saw the ocean he thought it was a wall of water standing straight up. Eventually he worked out his perspective, but the experience had a profound effect on him. He came to believe that it is impossible to see things truly until one understands what they truly are.

When Lucy saw something the size of a boot floating alongside the *Dawn Treader*, she couldn't tell that she was looking at the ship's shadow until she worked it out by relating its behavior to the shadow of a moving train. Only then could she see the ocean floor on which the shadow was cast. Without this revelation she would have been unable to see the fish-herdess who would become her friend in an instant. And yet when they reached the end of the ocean, they discovered it was bounded by a wall of water standing straight up. It's as if Lewis believed there could be a deeper truth in his initial vision.

Similarly, when Jill sees a group of giants standing in a trench, she has a moment of relief as she concludes that perhaps there aren't really giants at all in this country but only rocks that look like giants, until one of them, horribly, turns his head. Nor do the children make the connection between the Lady's brilliant green dress and the vision the owls reported Rilian having. Puddleglum ought perhaps to have guessed, but I suppose he would never have believed that finding the Prince would be that easy.

Aslan knew that the signs he made Jill memorize would look different when she got to them. As a matter of fact, the trio can hardly see at all as they arrive at the City Ruinous in the midst of a dreadful snowstorm. The main difference though between Aslan's mountain and the lonely lands north of Narnia is the presence of other voices, and other desires, than those Aslan lays out. So they struggle on right past their goal, ears frozen, eyes blind, fingers numb, wandering for a bit in the simple and pointless maze of "ME," and arrive at the gates of the giant castle.

Here Puddleglum starts to show his quality. He feels sure they've made the worst mistake possible, and this fact seems to give him courage, even a sense that he's in his element. He strides up boldly and calls for the porter, drinks what is offered to him, poison or no, and pretends (so he claims) to get drunk. "Resh-peckobiggle!" he cries, fearlessly and without a trace of irony (*SC*, chap. 8).

Inspired perhaps by Puddleglum's example, Jill herself begins to shine, helping their somewhat hopeless case by bursting into tears. She pretends to be a very little girl, coquettish and cloy-ingly sweet, and it has the most wonderful effect. They are fed and bathed and warmed, and indeed Harfang seems to be every-thing the Lady promised until Aslan shows up in a dream, not as a toy horse, nor even as a toy lion, but as a real giant lion who picks Jill up in his mouth and carries her to the window, where she can clearly see things for what they are.

What they are is three signs muffed, and only four to go by. Eustace and Puddleglum take their proper share of the responsi-bility, but only Jill has had the charge direct from Aslan, and only Jill has Aslan coming to her in a dream, so it's worse for her. Now they have to find some way to escape the giant's castle and get back to the place where they were most miserable the day before.

Eventually they escape the castle and find their way under the ruined city. With Aslan's help, they've been given a second chance at the third sign. We don't know what might have happened dif-ferently had they recognized the sign the first time around, and it might be tempting to conclude that it doesn't really matter, even that they got warm beds and good meals out of dawdling in the giant's castle, the danger of being eaten aside. But one awful thing could have been avoided by forgoing those pleasures: the horror of eating Talking Stag.

OBEDIENCE UNTO DEATH

Their journey through the Deep Realm is no more exciting than their journey across the moors. Although there are things well worth seeing here and there, all is sleepy and gray. There is no spark of wonder anywhere, just perhaps a quiet awe at times, like in a museum on a particularly dull school outing. "To your left is Father Time. He will awake at the end of the world."

After what seems like days and days in this gloom and drear, they arrive at a bustling city that is no more exciting than anything else they've seen. Then they come to a castle that is similarly drab until they enter and see the warm yellow glow of what might be a Narnian lamp and hear a human voice calling down to them, inviting them up and offering to tell them a story.

Fancy their still not making the connection, not suspecting that this young man is Rilian himself, under an enchantment. It could not be more obvious, and yet they don't see it at all, but only wonder (or Jill does) whether he might not be a bit silly, in the clinical sense. Her suspicion deepens as they sup together, listening to him prattle about the Queen and her plans for him to take over some country in Overworld.

They are an oddly frank bunch. The knight shows not the least hesitation about spilling his Lady's plans to strangers or telling them the whole truth, as far as he understands it, about his situation. The Witch (I mean Queen) evidently has too much faith in her magics to worry overmuch about who might blab what to whom, but then there usually aren't any people down there who would care.

In return, the children and Puddleglum are honest in their re-actions to this plan. Jill even goes so far as to aver that he will be a horrible tyrant, but he only laughs it off. Still, it's interesting that when Eustace mentions it'll be a bit rough on those he plans to attack, the man admits he had never considered it that way be-fore and looks just a little bit troubled before he laughs. He may be under an enchantment, but he has not lost the entirety of his noble nature.

In fact there is little real evil in him. It is with apparently gen-uine concern for their safety that he warns them about his con-dition during the hour of his enchantment, and from real loneli-ness that he asks them nonetheless to stay with him.

For all that they despise the young man, the adventurers take him at his word and believe that this is the one hour of his en-chantment. Even when he gives the fourth and final sign and charges them to release him in the name of Aslan himself, Eus-tace and Jill come up with perfectly serviceable rationalizations for why this might not be the true sign that Aslan intended. Pud-dleglum knows better: the fact that obeying the sign may end in their murder at the hands of a crazed man-serpent in no way lets them off the hook.

This is the crucible of obedience. If you understand and agree with the commands you've been given, it is no great virtue to obey them. But when the commands seem foolish or destructive, then whether or not you obey will largely be based on how much you trust (or fear) your commander. When you're not sure if you can see things for what they truly are, the only wise thing is to trust the commands of someone whose eyes are clear. If your commander is wrong, then your commander will bear the responsibility, but if your commander is right and you fail to obey, then the fault is entirely yours. Unfortunately, there is usually no way to distinguish between wise and foolish commands until the consequences of obedience or disobedience have played out.

Fortunately, once they have obeyed Aslan's sign, Prince Rilian is free and their mission is partway accomplished. But their safety is not yet guaranteed, for now they have the Witch to deal with. Far from being daunted by their swords and the destruction of the chair or disappointed by the foiling of her plans, she is ready to take them all on. A little fairy dust on the fire, a little strumming on the mandolin, a little logic, and she fully expects to blind them completely to anything resembling reality.

It's frightening how much sense her reasoning makes. Everything we think of as higher or better than Earth or Narnia can easily be explained away by suggesting that we take the little things we have and imagine them bigger and better. And what *does* the sun hang from? They debate as well as they are able, but no great enchantment is broken by argument alone. A sacrifice is generally required.

Puddleglum steps in with the heroic frying of his froggy foot. He admits that the Queen may not be wrong, that there's no denying her logic, but he chooses to believe that the people and the things in the world he may indeed have made up are infinitely more important than the things in the world the Witch has created. He vows to do his best to stay true to his own world, whether it exists or not, and to spend his life searching for it. It sounds stupid in a way, childish even, but it's enough to get the Witch as angry as a serpent, which gives them the opportunity to hack off her head without the impeachment to their honor that killing a woman would bring.

It is here, at the center of the Chronicles, when the adventure is at its most dreary and confusing, that make-believe is most potent and important.

When their victory results in the destruction of Underworld, Puddleglum once more is in his element. Flood, fire and foes are imminent, and the only apparent hope for escaping one is to succumb to another. The Prince, now that he's in his right mind, agrees with him. They make a formidable pair. The Prince fetches his shield and finds it no longer black but emblazoned with a lion, "'Doubtless,' said the Prince, 'this signifies that Aslan will be our good lord, whether he means us to live or die. And all's one, for that'" (*SC*, chap. 13). Puddleglum couldn't have said it better.

THE REWARD

They set out for the stables, hoping for nothing better than to make a grand ending but end up discovering that setting Rilian free has set all the gnomes free as well. Free from their workaday world, so familiar to many an urbanite, they've rediscovered their desire to sing and dance and shout and let off firecrackers. The witch's death has opened up the mouth of Bism, the true home of the gnomes, where salamanders speak from fiery rivers and diamonds grow on trees, in the warm heart of the world.

Once Golg (one of the gnomes) explains all this to the travelers, Rilian is faced with the same choice his father was decades earlier when he wished to abandon his kingdom to search for the end of the world. Which is more important, really? Should not wonder be sought out and enjoyed whenever the opportunity arises? Isn't that what it is to be childlike, and haven't we seen that childlike is good? Besides, they had given themselves up for dead already, as had most of Narnia, and who else would ever get the opportunity to explore the depths, the true Depths, of the world?

Maybe no one. Bism is not for Overlanders but for gnomes and salamanders, who do not need a visit from Prince Rilian to make their existence complete. All adventures in Narnia fulfill a purpose. Caspian went as far as he did toward the world's end in order to find nine lords who had been loyal to his father, and his reward was the hand of Ramandu's daughter in marriage. To go farther would have been to act on a mistaken notion that he deserved to see more. Since he was King, his life was not his own; his country needed him. The same holds true for Rilian, and besides, Jill is not likely to be convinced to go any deeper. She fears enclosed spaces as much as Eustace fears heights and has exhibited extraordinary courage in delving this far underground. Happily, Rilian sees sense and chooses to journey toward the adventures prepared for him in his own country.

It's a hard lesson. Our journeys, we feel, should be rewarded. We know Aslan would want to reward us, and here's his chance! We may not even be wrong. Oh, this is the really hard possibility:

What if God intended us to make the trip to Bism (or wherever), but we dawdled along the way, forgot or ignored the signs, and now there's no time? The King is dying, Narnia needs her King. Regret is a powerful emotion, and sometimes our only consolation is that there will be time for further adventures after we're dead, and that next time we'll listen better, obey more quickly and not be so thick-headed.

The point is, if we've accomplished the task for which Aslan sent us into Narnia, we have done well. If the best we can hope for is to come up out of the ground into a midwinter's dance of fauns and dwarfs, perhaps we can hardly complain. It's only in the moment that Bism presents itself, for a limited time, that desire and regret rise up to overwhelm us. The lure of the unexplored, of being discoverers and not just tourists, is grand and not to be scoffed at, but it is only one kind of adventure, and if that is the whole of our definition, then we will miss out on many more ordinary, common but no less magical adventures.

At last the sojourners arrive back in Narnia, and Eustace and Jill are treated to their own reward: a glimpse of the Narnia that the Pevensies knew and loved, where fauns dance by moonlight in the snow and dwarfs throw snowballs between them, where work is enjoyed because it is not considered work, where there's good, simple, hearty food and plenty of it, and where it's a little bit difficult to believe in Underland. Where all the fears and failures of their journey become worthwhile.

The following day they travel, not by air, as they did in getting to Narnia and in getting to the parliament of owls, not removed from the landscape, but on the backs of centaurs, right through the midst of the most beautiful parts of Narnia. It is perhaps a less comfortable method of transportation, but it is much more rewarding, and they never forget that journey.

When they get back to the castle of Cair Paravel, they watch from the fringes of the crowd as the aged Caspian blesses his son with his final breath. Their mission thus truly complete, they mention at last a desire for home. And then, from behind them, "I have come" (*SC*, chap. 16). Home has come. Aslan.

As so often happens in his presence, past mistakes come painfully and shamefully to mind. Jill wishes to confess all her mistakes and missteps and apologize for them, but before she can find the words, he touches their faces with his tongue and says, "Think of that no more. I will not always be scolding. You have done the work for which I sent you into Narnia." It's not quite the "Well done" he gave to Edmund at the end of *Prince Caspian*, but it's enough.

He blows them back to his Mountain, and they find Caspian there, lying dead in a stream. A drop of Aslan's blood revives him and makes him young again. At last he has arrived at the place his heart most desired when he was alive. He asks if it would be wrong to want a glimpse of Jill and Eustace's world, and Aslan says the most wonderful thing: "You cannot want wrong things any more, now that you have died, my son" (*SC*, chap. 16). Aslan grants Caspian's wish, breaking down the wall at the top of the hill behind Experiment House and lying down with his back to England while Caspian, Eustace and Jill ply the bullies with the flats of their swords and Jill's new riding crop. This leads to Eustace and Jill's deliverance from the horridness of that school, for Aslan is concerned with rescuing not only Narnians but schoolchildren in England as well.

The narrator finishes the story with the cruel admonition to the reader to be sure to visit the caves of Underland should he or she ever get to Narnia. But it's the adult part of me that calls it cruel. The child in me finds it hopeful: perhaps such a journey would not be impossible, even now. ❧

The Horse and His Boy

Before Shasta and his alleged father Arsheesh are visited by the Tarkaan with his singular horse, Shasta has no plan. He has had a hard and loveless life, and he harbors a yearning for something more, but he cannot act on that yearning because he does not even have a name for it. All he has is a direction: North.

Bree-hee-hinny-brinny-hooey-ha (or Bree as we shall henceforth call him) has more than a direction; he has memories of green fields and a happy foalhood. He knows what he yearns for, and when he meets Shasta, he recognizes that same yearning and formulates a plan: he and Shasta will run away.

Meanwhile, Aravis is formulating a plan of her own, also of escape, but hers involves more drastic measures. When Hwin, her horse, sees Aravis lift a dagger to her breast, the only plan the worthy mare can come up with is equally drastic: she puts her head between blade and flesh. When the immediate danger to Aravis's life is past, she formulates the same plan as Bree.

It seems an extreme coincidence that two captive Talking Horses should formulate the same plan at so nearly the same time that at one point they actually find themselves running side by side. Naturally each pair of fugitives wishes to increase the distance between the two, but in another extreme coincidence, two lions choose that moment to attack from either side, forcing the horses together.

Immediately a difference between horses and people becomes apparent. Two horses, seeing that they are both Talking Horses, want to join up with each other, for four is a much better herd than two, but two young people, seeing that they are both Talking People, would just as soon have nothing to do with each other, for they more clearly see their differences than their similarities. Fortunately, horse sense prevails.

A classic joke asks, "What's the quickest way to make God laugh?" The punch line answers, "Make a plan." I personally believe it's much easier than that to make God laugh, but the point is not without merit. The plans that Bree and Hwin and Aravis make are merely quick shots of courage, like shots of whiskey before a duel. Plans give one an illusion of control before all control is abandoned. Only Shasta (and Lucy before him) is content to float upon the currents of Providence and let them carry him where they will.

When the quartet reaches Tashbaan, Hwin comes up with another plan, this one intended to get them through the city unimpeded. It's a humble plan (but in a good way), and there's little doubt it would have worked had not Providence once more intervened.

First, Shasta's brother is already there, and the Narnians mistake Shasta for his twin, allowing him to overhear their plans and the best route across the desert. Immediately following Shasta's "capture," Aravis sees an old friend and is able to enlist her help in escaping the city, in the process of which she happens on a meeting between her intended fiancé, Ahoshta (the reason she had wanted to kill herself), the Tisroc and Rabadash, and overhears all their plans.

Some readers may choose to dismiss this string of coincidences that I have called Providence as nothing more than convenient plot devices. I agree that they are plot devices and that in a certain sense they may be convenient, but I refuse to dismiss them, because I believe that Aslan uses such devices frequently. I can't begin to explain what mechanism he uses to bring strangers together at propitious times, nor can I explain why some circumstances seem carefully orchestrated while the mass of events seems random. It's possible that the mass of events are really a string of coincidences so interwoven and convoluted that they only *seem* random. At any rate, I find it helpful to trust the storyteller when such questions arise.

THE CONSEQUENCES OF FREEDOM

Leading their flight across the desert, racing to stay ahead of Rabadash and his two hundred horses, Bree is confident that he knows his own limits and that they are the limits of a great warhorse. The narrator, however, avers that slavery robs one of the ability to motivate oneself. Had Bree lived his whole life in the free air of Narnia, he likely would have gloried in the strength of his legs and crested ridges as if they were the breakers of a rough sea and he a sturdy craft with the wind blowing full in his sails. Unfortunately he has been too long in Calormen, where work is drudgery and fun is defined as having nothing much to do, so he is ruled more by his limitations than by his potential. Fortunately, there is one present who has the will and means to motivate him, to teach him the further reaches of his potential. Her name is Hwin, and when she reaches her own limit, there is yet another. It is a humbling lesson for a horse who had thought himself more than a little above average.

Aslan's sudden appearance at the end of their race is nothing short of terrifying. Bree discovers that he is a much faster horse than Hwin (which comes as no surprise), but he also finds that when faced with a lion he has no thought for anyone but himself (which Shasta does). He is, after all, a seasoned warhorse. He swears (later on) that he never heard Shasta shout that they had to go back to save Aravis and Hwin, and the narrator graciously accepts him at his word. At any rate, his lapse gives Shasta the opportunity to learn the opposite, namely that he is the sort of person who will leap off a galloping horse and run unarmed toward a gigantic lion if his friends are in danger.

Amazingly, his mad rush seems to do some good, for though the lion tears Aravis, it doubles over as it does so and retreats in the face of such feckless valor. This is at least as amazing as Peter's slaying of the wolf, but Shasta gets even less thanks for his courage, as the hermit who takes them in mildly urges him to run as fast as he can out the opposite door for the chance to warn King Lune. And so Shasta is put to the same test as Hwin and Bree: finding out if he has the will to force his limbs beyond their endurance.

Through heat and flies and a stitch in his side, through the bewilderment of finding himself in a strange new land where he's expected to do things far more demanding than Arsheesh ever asked, he runs to a man he does not yet suspect is his father and gaspingly gives his warning. The delight with which King Lune greets him would have been a rich reward for all his labor had he the least indication that the delight was not intended for Corin.

At any rate, a life of slavery does not seem to have atrophied his will.

After the battle is won, Shasta finally learns the story of his life, as well as his true name. The boy who started off with no plan of his own finds out that his whole hard life has been part of a plan so grand that Aslan himself felt the need to intervene on more than one occasion. He has lived to fulfill a prophecy and thereby save his kingdom. In addition, he has rescued two Narnian Horses and won a bride. He has learned that Aslan's plans are long term, and not to be made sense of quickly.

THE RECKONING

When Aslan, mist enshrouded, listens to the list of Shasta's complaints, he says, "I do not call you unfortunate" (*HHB*, chap. 11).

It's hard for me to agree with him. Shasta (or Cor, as he will soon be called) grew up in virtual slavery, his escape was fraught with peril and privation, and now that the battle and his freedom are won, he is to be shouldered with the difficult responsibilities of a king. Although Aslan's plan was good for Archenland, it does seem a bit unfair to Cor.

It also seems unfair that after all the companions have been through they should have to face a reckoning regarding their performance. Bree has to face up to his failings and arrogance by being humbled once again when Aslan sneaks up behind him while he is declaiming his nonincarnational theology. He responds by scampering away in terror. Aravis has to suffer the pain of Aslan's scratches, which represent the lashes inflicted on her servant girl when Aravis ran away. It seems an uncharacteristically violent lesson in empathy, but she doesn't question it. She may question her father's authority to marry her off to someone she hates, but her only response to Aslan is "Yes, sir."

Her response is more gracious than Bree's, but Hwin's response is awe-inspiring. She alone has nothing to be ashamed of, but nevertheless she trembles violently as she trots toward Aslan. "'Please,' she said, 'you're so beautiful. You may eat me if you like. I'd sooner be eaten by you than fed by anyone else'" (*HHB*, chap. 14). What an extraordinary prayer. If we could only learn her attitude, and half her humility, we might be able to pray such prayers, and then we would truly be in Narnia.

Aslan's ultimate plan is not only to make us better people (or horses, or asses), but to enter into a union with us. Shasta and

Aravis don't exactly live happily ever after, but "they were so used to quarreling and making it up again that they got married so as to go on doing it more conveniently" (*HHB*, chap. 15). So Shasta does gain at least one fortunate thing from his travails. ✻

The Magician's Nephew

T he first time children from Earth go to Narnia, they jump in uninvited and bring with them unwelcome guests, so that evil enters yet another of Aslan's creations. You might think he'd get angry, maybe repent him of having made children, but he doesn't even stop what he's doing, so intent is he on finishing the good work that he began.

When the story opens, Digory has been taken from his home and his pony, his father is gone, he is living with a mad uncle, and his mother is dying. He is "so miserable that he didn't care who knew he had been crying" (*MN*, chap. 1). By the end of the story he has ridden a flying, talking horse, his father has come back, he has a new home in the country, bigger and more verdant than his old one, his mother has been healed, and his uncle, a little cured of his madness, has come to live with them. It seems almost as though the work that Aslan began was for the weal of this one boy. One of the glorious things about the story Aslan is telling in creation is that everyone is the main character.

This is an easy truth to grasp much of the time, for we naturally assume that we are the center of the universe, but it can be difficult to believe that the story God is telling puts us there as well. So often God seems intent on humbling us rather than glorifying us, or it can even seem as though he takes no thought for us whatsoever. This is the reason faith and hope abide, for without them we might never see the story through to the end that Aslan intends. Love also abides, but it does so for a higher purpose: not to show us that we are the main character in God's story, but that others are as well.

THE VALUE OF WAITING

Uncle Andrew fully accepts his place at the center and gets annoyed with Digory for constantly trying to shift the focus of his story away from him. He believes that "no great wisdom can be reached without sacrifice" (*MN*, chap. 2), but the sacrifices to which he refers are those of the creatures he has experimented on. He is ignorant (as is the Witch) of the higher truth that lives with Aslan: the only sacrifices that are worthwhile are those made by oneself for the sake of others.

Digory may not be so worldly-wise as his uncle, but he is less ignorant of Aslan's ways. When he understands the position Uncle Andrew has put him in, he willingly steps into the terrifying unknown to rescue Polly. His sacrifice is rewarded when he finds himself in a place where no action is required, where action is in fact nearly impossible. A lovely, peaceful, dreamy place: the Wood Between the Worlds.

This is a place so deeply contemplative that only trees can fully appreciate it. Mere children, such as Polly and Digory, find their minds so completely overwhelmed with serenity that there is little room for anything else. It is as if they have always been there and always will be there. No plans survive there long, for it is a place for simply being. If not for the guinea pig with a ring tied to a string around its belly, they might be there still.

From a certain perspective, it is unfortunate that the guinea pig happened by, for once the children's ability to plan is restored, Digory wants to explore other worlds. In this Digory is not entirely unlike his uncle. He thirsts for hidden knowledge, and although he is generally more thoughtful of others, he makes the same choice his uncle did when faced with a similar decision. In the same way that Andrew chose not to burn the box containing the Atlantean dust of which the rings are made, Digory chooses to twist Polly's wrist rather than allow her to restrain him from ringing the bell that wakes the Queen. He fails to grasp that it was not the burning question of what was in the Atlantean box that drove his uncle mad, but the pursuit of its secrets, which brought him into contact with "some devilish queer people and . . . some very disagreeable experiences" (*MN*, chap. 2). There are times when inaction is the better choice, even the more difficult and heroic choice.

The Queen of Charn chose to turn herself into a statue rather than submit to the difficulties of waiting, so that the time between uttering the Deplorable Word and her rescue seems to her instantaneous. As a result, she has no time to ponder the consequences of her action. Had she allowed herself that time, she might eventually have repented, for even witches can get lonely, if they let themselves, and loneliness, as Eustace found on Dragon Isle, can work profound changes in one's view of the world. Unfortunately, as is usual in the stories Aslan tells, we will never know what would have happened had she given herself that choice.

Once the Queen is awake, she has no time to waste. She wishes for more worlds to subdue, to make grand and if necessary to destroy. To get there, however, she must pass through the Wood Between the Worlds, where she turns white and becomes weaker than the children. In that place only one's essential self has meaning, and the Queen has become little more than her schemes and her knowledge and her desire for power. She sees no value in simply being, and as a result her being has atrophied to the point that she is nearly Nothing. I would venture to guess that Nothing is all evil is: it is that which has disobeyed Aslan's call to *be* and wishes the rest of creation to follow suit.

Polly and Digory get a small taste of what the Queen wished to avoid when they return to the world of Earth. Polly gets sent to her room for two hours, while Digory awaits the Queen's return at the window. Waiting is a dull business, made worse when every minute is amplified by watchfulness, but it is not without its own rewards. Digory overhears an offhand remark made by his Aunt Letty about fruit from the Land of Youth being all that could help Digory's mother. Ordinarily he would have assumed she didn't mean anything by it, but he knows now that other worlds exist. The hope that rises in his heart is so extreme he fights against it for fear that it will disappoint, as so many hopes have before. The two words *wait* and *hope* are very similar in the stories Aslan tells, and there is power in them.

One other character in the story has been waiting and hoping, but we have not met him yet. It would not even seem that the story has anything to do with him. He's only the cabby, after all, but in the melee that ensues upon the return of the Queen, he distinguishes himself as the bravest and kindest person present as he braves the Witch's wrath to try to calm his horse. His actions do not go unnoticed by the Storyteller.

THE JOY OF CREATION

When the tangle of people and horse and Witch descend into the second pool and land in a darkness the Witch describes as "Nothing," the Cabby creates a story to explain their situation, supposing them to have fallen into some diggings, perhaps for a subway station. He immediately finds something to be thankful for: no one has gotten hurt. He is able to hold a second story in his head simultaneously with the first one, which is that they may in fact be dead. But he is philosophical about even this contingency, for, as he says, "worse things 'appen at sea and a chap's got to die sometime. And there ain't nothing to be afraid of if a chap's led a decent life" (*MN*, chap. 8). He proceeds to burst into a song of the harvest.

Can you hear it? That's leadership for you, if you like. The Cabby's thoughts are all for the group, keeping them looking on the bright side, even while acknowledging the dark truth that they might be dead. He sings a harvest hymn in a place where nothing seems ever to have grown. Is it any wonder Aslan chooses him to be King?

Almost in answer, from far away comes the sound of another voice singing. There are no words—there's hardly a tune—and yet it seems a song of sowing and tending and reaping all at once. All of a sudden there is an accompanying chorus and a thousand thousand stars appear in the sky.

What follows is the most awesome sight I can imagine: Creation. The Witch and the Magician, who have braved horrors to seek magic, are aghast when they see it in its fullness. They want to leave, to kill the Lion who is showing them that all their power is paltry. The Cabby's response shows yet another of his qualities: in addition to bravery and kindness, selflessness and a good singing voice, he is humble. "'Glory be!' said the Cabby. 'I'd ha' been a better man all my life if I'd known there were things like this'" (*MN*, chap. 8). He has led a decent life up to this point, but he suddenly understands that "decent" isn't good enough by half in light of the true glory of creation.

All of us are meant to join in Aslan's song, be we stars or moles. If we cannot participate directly, we can at least heed the words of the Cabby: "Watchin' and listenin' 's the thing at present; not talking" (*MN*, chap. 9).

When Aslan is finished with his general creation, he falls silent himself for a moment and simply stares at those animals he has set apart. Under his scrutiny, the beasts that surround him are transformed into the sorts of creatures who could interact with a Talking Lion. With a flash of light and a long warm breath, Aslan gives them the power of speech, the ability to apprehend and respond. Once that is accomplished, Aslan addresses them with the most wonderful words a creator can impart: "'Creatures, I give you yourselves,' said the strong, happy voice of Aslan. 'I give to you forever this land of Narnia. I give you the woods, the fruits, the rivers. I give you the stars and I give you myself'" (*MN*, chap. 10). Aslan creates extravagantly and then freely gives it away. He does not wish for control or any more power than he already has. He wishes only for joy, for himself and for those he has created.

He then tells them what speech is for: "Laugh and fear not, creatures. Now that you are no longer dumb and witless, you need not always be grave. For jokes as well as justice come in with speech" (*MN*, chap. 10). This is not so much the case in the world of Earth, though it is still the ultimate goal. This world is full of sorrow; we have fallen from the original purpose of our creation. So in this world Jesus says, "Blessed are you who weep now, for you will laugh," but "Woe to you who are laughing now, for you will mourn and weep" (Luke 6:21, 25). Yet even here we may be comforted by the words of Ecclesiastes, that there is "a time to weep, and a time to laugh; a time to mourn, and a time to dance" (Ecclesiastes 3:4).

There are plenty of funny moments in the Chronicles of Narnia, but the most powerful moments are the ones that make me weep.

THE REWARDS OF VIRTUE

On the face of it, virtue is simple. The things Aslan asks are easy: "Narnia, Narnia, Narnia, awake. Love. Think. Speak. Be walking trees. Be talking beasts. Be divine waters. . . . Treat [the Dumb Beasts] gently and cherish them but do not go back to their ways" (*MN*, chaps. 9-10). Similarly, at the creation of Earth God commanded those made in his image: "Be fruitful and multiply, and fill the earth and subdue it; and have dominion over the fish of the sea and over the birds of the air and over every living thing that moves upon the earth" (Genesis 1:28), and "Of the tree of the knowledge of good and evil you shall not eat" (Genesis 2:17). These are commands that anyone would wish to obey and have no trouble doing so. Left to themselves, no one would think of disobeying.

Strangely, though, once the unthinkable has been suggested, it can seem like a matter of little real consequence. Certainly Digory, after agreeing to rescue Polly in spite of his uncle's machinations, and after braving the melee in front of his house to remove the Witch from the world of Earth, would not expect anyone to focus exclusively on the fact that he rang a small bell, or even that he twisted a little girl's wrist to do so. But that is what Aslan does. That one selfish act overshadowed all his other virtues, for it brought evil into Narnia on the day of its birth.

Aslan is very careful to make sure that Digory recognizes the truth about that act, the truth he already knows, which is that no one else can be blamed for that action, not Uncle Andrew's manipulations nor the enchantment claimed by the writing beneath the bell. Straying from the path of virtue, even a little bit, has disastrous consequences. We all know it. I won't presume to speak for you, but for myself, that knowledge does little to curb my disobedience.

Yet once the sin is confessed, Aslan does not dwell on it. The commands he gives for atonement seem all but impossible, but in truth they are little harder than his original injunctions. It is our own failures that make us weaker than we were created and that make a return to the path of virtue so difficult. Aslan knows this. He knows it is difficult for Digory, and he shares his sorrow concerning his mother. He is sadder even than Digory, and Lord of all creation though he may be, he speaks intimately with this little boy, telling him that only the two of them yet know Grief in Narnia. "Let us be good to one another," he says (*MN*, chap. 12), and the image of the tears shining in the Lion's eyes sustains Digory throughout his quest.

In truth, Aslan does little in the way of command. He asks. He asks the Cabby if he would like to stay in Narnia forever and be its king. In response to the one hesitation, he summons the Cabby's wife with one long, low note. Polly "felt sure that it was a call, and that anyone who heard that call would want to obey it and (what's more) would be able to obey it, however many worlds and ages lay between" (*MN*, chap. 11). He asks Polly if she has forgiven Digory for the violence done her in the Hall of Images and then asks Digory if he is ready to undo some of the damage his action has caused. Over Digory's objection, he says, "I asked, are you ready"? (*MN*, chap. 12).

The risk one faces when choosing to ask for help instead of commanding it is that one or more respondents may refuse. The tasks Aslan asks are crucial, and the individuals he asks are uniquely qualified to do them. The quest he bestows on Digory is for the protection of Narnia, but it will be dreadfully difficult for one small boy to undertake. So he asks Strawberry if he would like to be a winged horse, and further, if he would consent to carry Digory and Polly to the garden that is Digory's destination.

Notice that Aslan gives Strawberry wings and a new name before asking his help. It might seem wiser to ask help first and make the transformation contingent upon an affirmative response, but Aslan gives as freely as he asks. Strawberry had been a slave in his old life, forced to pull something heavy and black behind him. Now he is Fledge, and he is free even of gravity. He is also free to say no to Aslan's request. Had he done so, perhaps some other creature would have stepped forward to say yes. Barring that, Digory would perhaps have managed the trek on his own two feet. Fortunately for him, Fledge is willing to ease his journey. The only hard part left for Digory is to face temptation a second time.

FACING TEMPTATION

Whether or not there was any magic surrounding the pedestal on which the bell in Charn sat, it was nothing compared to the enchantment produced by the sight and smell of the apples on the green hill far to the west of Narnia. By the power of their goodness, their native virtue, these apples cause terrible hunger and thirst. Digory finds the strength within himself to withstand the strong temptation to eat even before he notices the Phoenix roosting in the treetop, but having mastered the voices in his own mind, he is immediately faced with the Witch's.

Her first attempt at temptation has little effect, for Digory has no desire to live forever and rule by her side. Children are less likely than adults to have this sort of desire, for old age seems far away and mortality is little more than a concept. It is a clumsy opening, but I think the Witch has more than Digory in mind when she makes the offer. Having gained for herself eternal youth, she must realize that she cannot now pass the time, as she did on Charn, in limbo. Now she will have to endure the slow pace of time, and for the first time she gives thought to the problem of loneliness. Her second stab, however, cuts to Digory's heart.

What if, asks the Witch in essence, you stray from virtue for the sake of someone else? A quick trip to Earth, and Digory's mother will be healed. He has no answer to this and forbears only because he realizes that the Witch must have some ulterior motive, since she obviously has no real concern for his mother's welfare. Still, the question gives him pause, and were it not for the memory of Aslan's tears, he might really have gone mad from wondering what might have happened.

Although the trek has required little physical effort on Digory's part, Aslan's "Well done" shakes the ground: a little boy has bested the destroyer of Charn.

Aslan's plans take time, and when they are sidetracked or derailed by sin, he is content to let them take longer. He desires only joy for his creation and is rather saddened than angered by those like the Queen and Uncle Digory who refuse to enter into that joy because of impatience and a belief that there is only one real main character in all the worlds. As Aslan tells Digory: "All get what they want: they do not always like it" (*MN*, chap. 14). ❧

The Last Battle

We know enough about Aslan by now to guess that although he may not have looked like a lion at the time, it is no other than he who created Charn. The value of that reddish-gray desolation is to illustrate the awful truth that endings are not happy perforce. Aslan is powerful enough to create worlds and redeem sinners, but on Charn evil won out. One single person destroyed a world Aslan created good, and survived to travel to another world even as Aslan was in the midst of creating it.

Remember the Hall of Images in *The Magician's Nephew*? At one end of the hall the faces were "kind and wise," but as one progressed the faces became first solemn, then strong and happy but cruel, then more cruel, then no longer happy, then finally the White Witch herself. Compare this progression to the parade of characters we have met in Narnia. Is there a similar pattern? Perhaps the line is not so straight between "kind and wise" and cruel. But certainly there is a stark contrast between the first animals—the Jackdaw who made (or was) the first joke, Fledge, an old horse made new—and the last animals: Shift the selfish, manipulating Ape, and Puzzle the Ass who lets him get away with it. Faithfulness has not died in Narnia, as perhaps it had in Charn, and the King is still worthy of the name, but a canker has taken root in the land, and the animals no longer clearly recollect who Aslan truly is.

Shift is evil in a way that is new to Narnia. Fenris the wolf served the White Witch. Nikabrik championed the rights of dwarfs. Shift serves no one but himself and is clever enough to convince others to serve him as well. He is perhaps the first true Narnian to truly resemble the foreign-born Witch. The Witch, in her own world, was selfish enough to put her world to an end when it stopped serving her purpose. Shift is not so powerful, but his cleverness and conceit set in motion the events that lead directly to Narnia's end. If Jewel's analysis is correct, Shift betrayed all of Narnia to the Calormenes and perhaps had intended this even before he found means in the lion skin.

In these latter days, my desire is that of the good creatures of Narnia: I want to see Aslan, who is called Jesus. I want to see his face. O and I want him to love and accept me. I will have difficulty enough facing him without my knees knocking together; if the burden he brings is heavy I may well collapse.

This is the situation the denizens of Lantern Waste find themselves in when Shift unveils his rendition of Aslan, one made in his own selfish image. Although it is nothing more than an Ass in a fur coat, everyone knows that Aslan is "not a tame lion" and he has been kinder to them than they deserved in the past, and it's more than likely that his mercy has come to an end. Thank God that's not true, and never will be, but when you long to see Aslan and someone presents you with him, presents you with the object of your desire, how can you then complain that he's not the lion you wanted him to be? Who are we to judge the King?

I hope you will not be offended when I suggest that Aslan might not be offended by the image of himself as an Ass in a fur coat. Nor Jesus either. We know they're not ashamed to appear as lambs. Isn't the wearing of a lion's skin a good metaphor for "putting on the new man" (Colossians 3:10—being "clothed . . . with the new self"; cf. Ephesians 4:24)? Pretending to be Jesus is not far from what Jesus would like us to do. Puzzle performs the charade in all humility, suffering in it, just as Jesus put on flesh and suffered in human skin. People in our world use his image for all manner of selfish ends, but in the ultimate end, Puzzle enters the stable with recognition. Though we don't know what Aslan says to him, we do know that he is allowed to stay.

Puzzle does what Jesus urged on the Sermon on the Mount: he does not resist the evildoer. He does not ever imagine that he is anyone special. He has everything Shift lacks, and Shift has the temerity to believe he is cleverly using the simple donkey.

Poor Shift! Had he once done something purely for Puzzle's sake, as Puzzle tirelessly does everything Shift asks of him, Shift might have hoped to escape his fate at the beak of Tash. He had every opportunity to learn the folly of his way, even to the point of being put in Puzzle's hooves and cruelly used by Rishda Tarkaan. If only he had once used Puzzle as a model, he might have made it. If just once he had realized that Puzzle was truly the better of the two, he might have learned the error of his cleverness.

He thought he could use the gods for his own profit. He thought he could twist the stories, the very idea of stories, so that instead of following them to the deeper truths they represent, he could take control of them and force others to follow his lies so that everyone would serve him. The result was an example of the greatest evil that one creature can commit upon others: by twisting true stories, he opened up the possibility that the true stories might be lies as well. The dwarfs were not entirely foolish to arrive at the conclusion that they did.

Every day people twist the true stories, using that which was meant to be good in order to do evil, that is, to satisfy their own desires. And not even their true heart's desires, but the banal desires of their bellies. How does one convince someone who has seen through the lies of one of these tale tellers, someone who has never met Aslan, that the other stories, the true stories, which also demand service and sacrifice, are real even though the others are damnable lies? The only way I know of is to live the life of service and sacrifice that is demanded by the true stories, to be a model of what I'm preaching. But that, as often as not, will leave me looking like Puzzle, which is a terrible thing for anyone with an ounce of pride to imagine.

I don't mean to suggest that Puzzle is perfect. As with most people, his greatest strength is startlingly similar to his greatest weakness. As Eustace starts to say, "If you'd spent less time saying you weren't clever and more time trying to be as clever as you could . . ." Strength in oneself and the courage to have one's own convictions are good things, vital things. Having the heart of a servant does not mean saying yes to everyone who asks for something.

But these are obvious observations, and as helpful as Eustace's admonition. The better response is Jill's: "'Oh leave poor old Puzzle alone,' she said. 'It was all a mistake; wasn't it, Puzzle dear?' And she kissed him on the nose" (*LB*, chap. 8). We need to have grace on each other, just as Aslan has grace on each of us. We may not know what Aslan says to Puzzle when the two finally meet, but we see his ears droop at first and then perk right up again. He has kept his heart and never once used Shift as a model to think that he deserved service from others. He has kept his own self pure, and sometimes that is heroic enough.

PREPARING FOR BATTLE

How little I have talked about battle in this book! All the Chronicles except *The Magician's Nephew* feature battles in which blood is spilled (and even *The Magician's Nephew* had the melee at the lamppost), and yet I have hardly said a word about this more usual arena of heroism. According to Roonwit the Centaur, "Noble death is a treasure which no one is too poor to buy" (*LB*, chap. 8). Noble death is what Christianity is all about. In this it differs hardly at all from other of the world's religions, but it's a point that's easily lost in all the *How shall we then live?* questions. The simple answer to all such questions is, *In such a way that we will be well prepared to die.*

Battle is ugly, and people die in it. In our world, people like Gandhi and Martin Luther King Jr. have espoused a paradigm of nonviolent confrontation that is both laudable and effective. It is the picture I mentioned earlier of grasping the enemy's sword from the wrong end, and yet the Narnia narrator seems to aver that there comes a time when grasping your own sword by the hilt is not inappropriate. As Jill says, "I'd rather be killed fighting for Narnia than grow old and stupid at home and perhaps go about in a bathchair and then die in the end just the same" (*LB*, chap. 9).

My own views and actions tend toward a pacifist response to aggression, and yet there is undeniably a surge in my heart when I read about battle. Lewis does not romanticize bloody conflict in the Chronicles of Narnia. Indeed, the words of the bear as he dies are heart-wrenching: "I—I don't—understand" (*LB*, chap. 11). Where Jill has to turn her head away to keep from wetting her bowstrings, I have to turn my head to avoid wetting the pages.

War kills, and even the enemy is somebody's friend, and so I am repulsed by it. Yet it gives everyone involved in a conflict the opportunity to lay their life on the line for what they believe in. As Tirian cries as he steps out from behind the stable when he sees the Calormenes advancing upon the boar and no one stepping forward to intervene: "Here stand I, Tirian of Narnia, in Aslan's name, to prove with my body that Tash is a foul fiend, the Ape, a manifold traitor, and these Calormenes, worthy of death" (*LB*, chap. 10). I wish I could have been there to fight and die at his side.

BEYOND THE TITLE PAGE

The Last Battle contains an awful lot of theology. When I was in high school and a friend told me the Chronicles of Narnia were all Christian allegory, *The Last Battle* was the only one I would concede might have Christian overtones. Nowadays (obviously) I find all kinds of Christian considerations throughout the Chronicles, but the ones I find most intriguing are those surrounding the stable.

It starts with "the nonsense about Tash and Aslan being the same" (*LB*, chap. 4). The only way I can make sense of such a statement, substituting Jesus for Aslan and Tash for any other god, is by taking Ginger the cat's stance: the only way Jesus or Aslan could be the same as any other god is if neither in fact exists.

I read a sermon from a Unitarian church wherein the speaker made a case for the Goddess as an older and more peaceful higher power than the warlike male God of monotheism. When in the course of the sermon she hypothesized the origins of the Goddess, she supposed that earlier societies were matriarchal and that when a matriarch was asked how the world was created she would naturally refer to a Great Mother's giving birth to the world. In other words, the speaker saw religion as a reflection of society, the expression of a worldview, and nothing more.

Now, I am woefully inadequate to make generalizations about world religions. Further, of course it's hardly fair to form a conclusion about any belief system based on one sermon. One might as well base one's understanding of Christianity solely on the Chronicles of Narnia. Here I am more concerned with the Unitarian idea that all religions are equally valid than I am with those who worship the Goddess. Judaism, Islam, Buddhism, Hinduism, B'hai, shamanism, pantheism, ancestor worship—all have their value as belief systems, and Christianity has its problems, in practice if not in theory, since not one of us is worthy of the name. But the one thing Christianity has that transcends "belief systems" is the belief that the Creator of the world was born of a human woman, died at the age of thirty-three, rose from the dead and sent his Spirit to bring all who call on him into his presence.

It's a difficult belief to maintain, and there plenty who call themselves Christian who do not take it strictly literally. But if it is not literally true, then the Unitarian sermon has it right, and the only valid way to judge a religion is to judge the society in which it holds sway. If Aslan is a real Lion, however, then the only judgment a person or a society need worry about is his judgment of them.

That judgment comes on the other side of the stable door. In the meantime, we must contend with the overwhelming question of what Aslan is truly like. When Tirian hears that Talking Horses are enslaved and Talking Trees are being cut down on Aslan's orders, he says, "Would it not be better to be dead than to have this horrible fear that Aslan has come and is not like the Aslan we have believed in and longed for?" (*LB*, chap. 3). Accordingly he offers the hilt of his sword to the Calormenes in order to put himself at the mercy of Aslan, whoever he really is. Such trust is madness unless one truly believes that Aslan is the ultimate judge.

Even given his belief, it might seem a bit naive as far as strategies are concerned, yet it proves the quickest way to solve the mystery of the apparent change in Aslan's personality. Had Tirian not been bound to a tree all night, he might never have called on the children from the far world of Earth who had helped Narnia so many times before. Things might have turned out much worse had he not been so precipitous and humble in his guilt over slaying the unarmed Calormenes who were driving the Talking Horse.

Yet this is the mystery: we are called to fight the battle against evil, to join the right side and fight with all our might, but it is inherently a losing battle. There is no triumph at the end. All who stay to fight the last desperate battle outside the stable are either killed or thrown through the terrible door. We are called to fight, and we are called to lose. We are called to fight by losing. Only thereby are we judged worthy to enter into the paradise that exists within the stable.

This explains, at least to some extent, why Emeth is welcomed into Paradise. He, like Hwin, would rather face the wrath of the one he worshiped than receive any good thing from anyone else. Tash is incapable of receiving such purity of heart.

But it doesn't explain everything. The dwarfs fought to win Narnia for themselves, and yet they also are welcomed into the true Narnia beyond the stable. Aslan even puts before them a royal feast, yet they are unable to experience any of the wonderful things that the others are reveling in because they have closed their minds to hope and beauty and truth. They have become like Uncle Andrew, who was so good at convincing himself that animals can't talk that he was finally unable to understand them.

It seems, at least in Narnia, that the only criterion for entrance into a glorious afterlife is whether when you meet Aslan face to face you respond in fear and hatred or with fear and love. I don't know if the same will hold true when this world ends, but it seems to me possible, in the light of what I have learned from *The Last Battle*, that the War on Earth was lost the moment the Lord Adam and the Lady Eve transgressed God's single prohibition. Rather than give up and scrap the whole project, though, God has kept battling, for thousands of years so far, to save those who could be still be saved.

Narnia, then, is one more means to that end, both in the narrative and perhaps also in the strictly literal sense. It would again explain why Aslan is always sending children into the most dangerous, difficult and desperate adventures. It is so they can get to know him in a place where the air is pure and relatively uncluttered, where the stakes are not so ambiguous as they often seem in this world. In Narnia the mission is always clear: rescue. In rescuing, the children are themselves on the road to being rescued. In reading, we who are not (so far as we know) make-believe are shown this road. Lewis and Jesus have collaborated to create Narnia so that those of us who read the Chronicles might have a slightly better chance of loving Jesus when we encounter him, of recognizing that he and Aslan are truly the same, and that although we may be filled with fear and trembling in his presence, we have come to know him too well for fear to overwhelm our love. ✄

Afterword

I am told there is a lion who wants to meet with me, but I'm having trouble finding him. I had thought he was in Narnia, but it turns out that's only where his shadow lives. The real Aslan is larger and more complex, unconstrained by book covers. The true Aslan is off in the woods just over there, beckoning.

I see him.

I see him there, but I don't respond.

Why don't I respond? Am I scared? Too grown up? Too prideful, sinful, willfull? Am I stupid? I continue on my way, the way that looks the best to me, and I make believe, I use the huge imagination he has given me, to look right through him as if he wasn't there at all.

Aslan, I pray, *hear my call. Save me from the prison of my self. Please, Aslan, we need you. Hear our call.*

All the time he beckons, patient as a cat on the prowl, waiting for one of us to turn to him with joy and welcome, like a child who catches sight of a trusted friend.

I knew a cat once, a stray whom I called Fernando. He modeled to me better than any story the kind of joy and welcome I believe Aslan longs for from us.

At the time I was living on the second floor of a three-story apartment building that faced a mirror image of itself across a narrow parking lot. Each floor was fronted by a long balcony that connected a staircase at both ends. Several times a day I would go out to the balcony to enjoy a cigarette and survey the parking lot.

The first time I saw Fernando he was slinking among the cars. He was thin to the point of starvation, and he was so muddy that it was impossible to determine the color of his fur. In spite of this condition, he had the gift of disappearing in a blink. When I walked down to offer my assistance, he ran away. Slowly, with a casual air, taking care to make no sudden movements, I wandered in the direction he had dashed, but there was no sign of him. I got down on my hands and knees to scan beneath the cars, but I saw no hint of a cat. Nevertheless, I left a can of tuna next to one of the dumpsters and returned to my balcony. From there I watched him emerge from the opposite direction from which I was sure I had seen him run and sniff at the tuna. A minute later it was gone. He disappeared again while I replaced it, and he ate half the second can as well.

After that I took to buying dry cat food and leaving a bowlful outside my door every night. In the mornings it would always be gone. Occasionally I would see him prowling about, and I was happy to note that he gradually grew sleek and strong and orange, but he still wouldn't trust me to approach him.

I don't remember the first time he let me pet him, but once he took that step of faith, he never hesitated to approach me and to twine about my legs as I smoked. Or he would sit beside me, gazing out over the parking lot like a lion embodying a noble definition of pride.

One day in particular sticks in my memory. Fernando was walking down from the third story, making his rounds (I wasn't the only one who left him food). When he reached my balcony he caught sight of me, and for an instant he was still, his eyes inscrutable. Suddenly his front paws lifted off the concrete till he was half standing as he surged forward, his back legs outpacing his front in his haste to come greet me. Rarely in my life have I felt so loved.

I wish my response to Aslan could be similar in spirit if not in form. Aslan has been leaving cans of tuna for me for a long time now, and I have grown plump and sated on his tender chunks of fish, but I have yet to let go my mistrust of him. He seems friendly enough, but he's so big and dangerous-looking that it's hard to be sure. He's very patient, and his voice is quiet and sweet, which makes me think he's stalking me, preparing to pounce, so I run. Even if he doesn't want me for dinner, he might want to capture me as a pet, to keep me cooped up inside his house where the air doesn't move and the smells are always the same. If I could know for sure that all he wants to do is scratch behind my ears and under my chin and sit with me every now and again, I'd welcome him with the same joy Fernando expressed to me. But reports on him vary (in this world at least), and I've got some freedom to enjoy before I give him any advantage that he might use against me.

If I could find some good use for my freedom, I might be happier with it.

I had intended to end this book with an addendum to the Chronicles of Narnia, a short story that followed Susan into another adventure. Had she been a real girl in the 1940s she would be in her sixties now, and surely she would be lonely. Her whole family died in a train crash, after all, and this was after she had forsaken her friendship with Narnia. Wouldn't it be wonderful, I thought, if Aslan would give her another chance, would show her, once more, what he desires for her?

One reason you're not reading this story is that it is without question an infringement of copyright. A little research by one of the editors at IVP revealed the existence of at least three other stories with the same premise, full-length, unpublished books concerning Susan. The fact that these books exist suggests that I am not alone in my anxiety. It seems unthinkable that someone like Susan, who had actually been to Narnia, who had lived for years and years as a queen in Narnia, should turn her back on it in the end.

My incredulity is belied by several examples in Scripture. Adam and Eve are the most obvious ones, but there's also Gideon, who after defeating the Midianites with just three hundred men, worshiped idols. Saul, the first king of Israel, turned his back on God and, when God stopped talking to him, turned to a medium to raise the spirit of his mentor Samuel, who rebuked him. Jesus spoke of those from whom seven spirits had been cast out, only to have the spirits gather allies and return, so that the last state of the person was worse than the former.

I cannot speak for the other writers of Susan stories, but I confess my own motivation for writing her back into Narnia was selfish: I wanted to be comforted in my disobedience.

As the Pevensies trudged with Trumpkin through the forest in the wrong direction, only Lucy could see Aslan beckoning from the trees, showing them the right path. It made no sense to go in his direction other than the fact of his beckoning, so Lucy was voted down. It was not until the more sensical path led them into arrows and enemies that they turned back and found Aslan still waiting. Then Susan told Lucy that she had believed her sister's vision from the start, deep down, but had not wanted to follow.

That's where I am now. All I can hope for is a failure on the road of my choosing that will chase me back to surrender to Aslan's will. Experience has shown that such a failure will indeed befall me, but what I long for is to be as truehearted as a Beaver or a Badger, or even a stray cat, and it irks me to find I cannot, of my own volition, be such. It scares me to think that my condition might become permanent. In writing a story about Susan's redemption, I had hoped to make it my own.

Instead I wrote another story, whose protagonist is of a similar age and temperament as Susan, and who is reading the Chronicles of Narnia for the first time. I wanted to observe her reaction to Susan's absence from the land inside the stable. Along the way, as so often happens in stories both real and imagined, the character developed a life of her own.

👑

Playing Narnia

Recently retired from the United States Postal Service, Suanne Ashe missed the structure of an eight-to-five workday but didn't waste any time feeling sorry for herself. She had worked through the anthrax scares that followed the attack on the World Trade Center and was glad to be free of the almost constant anxiety that had subsequently accompanied her job. In those days the Chronicles of Narnia had not yet been made into a series of Disney films, but word of the upcoming movies had incited a great deal of excitement in Suanne's grandson, Ryan, who insisted she read the books before the movies came out.

"Gran'ana, there's lions and dragons and giants and ships and a witch and, and, and stars," Ryan had said. "Stars that are really people. So you've gotta read it."

"Are there pandas?" she had asked, hoping to sound droll. "I like pandas."

"No, Gran'ana, there's no pandas."

"Are there Archaeopteryxes? Platypuses, marmosets, lemurs?" she said, smiling now.

"No, Gran'ana. What's a lemur?"

"It's a little monkey, like you."

"Gran'ana!"

As a rule, Suanne did not care for fantasy. She preferred biographies and memoirs, stories about real people living in the real world. Nevertheless, for the sake of her grandson she walked to the local bookstore, wasted a good deal of time searching in the science fiction/fantasy section before being directed to the young adult shelves, found a paperback set, was appalled by the price, was even more appalled by the price of the hardcover set, and consoled herself with the thought that she could give it away when she was finished before taking it to the counter, paying for it and walking home.

Despite the cost, she found a sliver of excitement lodging in her bosom. As she walked, her excitement grew. She was glad that her husband, Bill, wasn't home when she got back, so that she could tear off the cellophane in peace. Sitting on the edge of Bill's recliner, she opened up *The Magician's Nephew* and began to read.

A few pages in, the character of Polly gave her an idea, which was absurd but she nonetheless acted upon it. She pulled a two-liter bottle of ginger ale out of the refrigerator and carried it, along with the books, upstairs, where she pulled the cord that lowered the ladder that led to the attic. She had not been up there since she and Bill moved in some fifteen years ago. It was a triangular space, the roof coming to a point in the middle and the slant reaching all the way down to the floor. Pink insulation was fastened between the bare rafters. She and Bill did not even use the attic for storage, and it was a bit too warm, but she found a relatively comfortable seat on a few boards not far from the bare bulb that hung from the roof. The place was just rustic enough to allow her to believe she was a little girl reading an adventure tale at the end of the nineteenth century.

Several hours later, when she heard a door open downstairs, she felt suddenly sheepish. She wasn't sure that Bill would understand the impulse that had sent her up there. Indeed, she wasn't sure she understood it herself.

As silently as she could, her heart pounding unaccountably, she crept to the trapdoor and descended. She heard Bill's footsteps heading toward the staircase as she slid the bottom half of the ladder into the top half and lifted the trapdoor closed. She had left the light on, she realized, and the books, and, most disappointingly, the pop, but there was nothing to be done about it now. Scurrying into the bedroom as Bill ascended, she strove to slow her breathing and gather her composure as she busied herself tidying.

"Here you are," said Bill. "Have you seen my reading glasses? Hank gave me a new contract to look over, and without my goggles the fine print is going to give me a migraine." He waved a sheaf of papers at her as he cast his eyes about the room with a look of befuddled concentration that normally irritated her but now made her want to laugh.

"I think I saw them on top of the refrigerator this morning," she said.

"The refrigerator?" he echoed. Then his eyes lit up, and he raised one finger. "Oh yes!"

She could not remember the last time she had felt such fondness for him. Over the next few days, as she spent more and more time in the attic and in Narnia, she found that her attitude toward Bill was not the only thing that was changing. She was developing what she came to think of as Narnian eyes.

She had always gone on walks in the mornings, but now the walks were lasting longer, and she was noticing things that had never caught her attention before. It was as if she had never truly understood the color green, or the beauty of the color gray. The air was surely not Narnian, but she breathed it deeper and noticed more of its aromas. Sometimes the predominant smell was sewer, but other times it was fresh-mown grass or lilac. Even the shrill trill of the cicadas sounded musical to her.

She could not say for sure that the Chronicles of Narnia were solely responsible for this change. Perhaps it had as much to do with the fact that she was keeping them a secret from her husband, or perhaps it was simply increased exercise, but she couldn't deny that she was enjoying the Chronicles immensely.

Her son Jeffrey, Ryan's father, had loved fantasy stories as a child, and Suanne had always tried to discourage him, fearing that he would turn inward and get lost in his imagination. It was true that he was hopelessly irresponsible, late with his bills and rarely remembered to call his mother unless he needed something. But in Susan Pevensie, one of the four children in *The Lion, the Witch and the Wardrobe* and *Prince Caspian,* she found someone who could manage both a sense of wonder in the fantastic and a practicality of which Suanne approved. Perhaps because of the similarity in their names, Suanne became very attached to Susan Pevensie and thought about her often, almost as if they had been childhood friends.

Alone among her brothers and sister, Susan had seen the ne-
cessity of taking coats from the wardrobe as they all entered the
Narnian winter on their first visit, and it was she who convinced
them of the madness of leaving their shoes on the beach on their
second. Suanne thought it was horribly unfair that Aslan deemed
Susan too old to return to Narnia at the end of her second visit.

Her disappointment at the absence of Susan soured her experience of *The Voyage of the Dawn Treader,* so much so that she almost
stopped reading. It was such a dark story, with children being
sold as slaves, the boy Eustace being turned into a dragon and
one of the Lords they were looking for being found at the bottom of a lake, having been turned into solid gold some years before. She could almost sympathize with Eustace, who at least was
able to keep his feet firmly planted in reality through all of this,
even if after a while it was a bit stupid of him to insist on believing there could be a British consulate anywhere within a million
miles of that ship. She was annoyed with Lewis's obvious dislike
for Eustace and felt he was purposely painting a ridiculous picture of him, when really the underlying things he was insisting on
were eminently reasonable.

The invisible Monopods were the last straw. Sitting in her attic, drinking too much ginger ale, reading about those ridiculous
little gnomes . . . "It's disgusting," she said aloud, and wondered
if her fears about the effects of fantasy on Jeffrey's mind had been
justified after all. The attic was hot, as usual, and the board she
was sitting on was making her bottom numb—she suddenly
couldn't believe she had ever thought it all exciting and fun. "I'm

turning into a crazy old lady," she scolded, speaking, apparently, to the book and shaking it. She almost put it down, never to pick it up again, but a voice, or words anyway, from somewhere in the back of her mind said, "Finish it."

She shifted her position slightly, holding out one leg that had fallen asleep, and wondered if the voice were all the proof she needed that she had indeed lost her mind. Nevertheless, as she waited for the pins and needles to subside, she finished the chapter about Dufflepuds and turned to a chapter called "The Dark Island." It did not sound promising, but she decided to give it one more chance before turning her back on fantasy for good. The chapter turned out to be worse than all the rest of the book put together, as the ship and its crew foolishly sailed into an un-natural and entirely avoidable darkness in the middle of the ocean, shamed into it by a Mouse. It turned out to be a place where nightmares came true.

She was quite certain she didn't want to read any further, but as the ship circled, trying to get out, its crew in a panic, Suanne began to feel the world of the book and the world wherein she was reading the book come together. The fictional characters' frantic attempts to row themselves out of the darkness had the same quality as her vain attempts to put down the book.

Her eyes were wide with horror by the time she came to Lucy's prayer: "Aslan, Aslan, if ever you loved us at all, send us help now," and though she had never really believed in a personal God, she felt the prayer echo in her mind. And suddenly she was so deeply into the story that her panic eased just a little. When the albatross spoke to Lucy as it flew by the crow's nest, "Courage, dear heart," a stab of joy and relief pierced her heart, and she read on hungrily, hopelessly lost in the fantasy.

By the time the *Dawn Treader* passed the last island and Eustace, Edmund and Lucy were disembarking with Reepicheep at the End of the World, Suanne's eyes hurt from the brightness, and the light that presaged the Lamb seemed almost to strike her blind. She was no longer seeing black type on a white page but only the unbearable glare of the Silver Sea. When the Lamb turned into a Lion and told Lucy and Edmund they wouldn't be returning to Narnia, she could hear Lucy's voice, in between sobs, imploring, "It isn't Narnia, you know, it's *you*. We shan't meet *you* there, and how can we live, never meeting you?"

Closing her eyes, Suanne hugged the book to her chest and breathed, "Yes. Yes, dear, I know." She breathed in the warm attic air and sighed. "How *can* we live?" Hardly daring to hope this tiny book could provide a satisfactory answer to the question that seemed to have existed deep in her heart her whole life, she turned her attention back to the words on the page and read Aslan's answer: that he was in Lucy's world as well, and they must learn to know him by a different name.

The next day was a Sunday, and Bill left early to go golfing with some of his buddies, so Suanne went to church alone, as she often did during the summer, but this time she went with a new sense of anticipation. She was convinced that Aslan's name in this world was Jesus, and Aslan had become so real to her that she was all but certain that she would meet him in his church, if she looked for him. She sang the hymns, listened to the Scripture readings, paid attention to the sermon and was disappointed to find that there was no magic in any of it to rival what she had experienced on board the *Dawn Treader*. When it came time for Communion, she walked down the aisle woodenly, feeling as if she was in line for bread in Cold War Russia. She had been duped into believing something that simply wasn't true. *Oh, but I so wish it were*, she thought, as she cupped her hands to receive a tiny crust of bread.

As she walked from the priest to the chalice bearer, she lifted her cupped hands to her mouth, pushed the crumb past her lips and bit down. In an instant her whole body was awash with a sensation that she was never able, after, to describe. ("It would just sound hokey," she would say.) A dull, remote pain was her only clue that she had fallen to her knees. She looked up at the cross that hung before the glorious stained-glass window.

"Oh. Hello," she said.

She could hardly bring herself to swallow the morsel as someone, an acolyte perhaps, helped her to her feet and started to lead her to a pew. She pulled away from him. "I want to taste the wine," she said, though the words sounded indistinct to her ears, and she was staggering to the rather alarmed-looking chalice bearer. She grasped the cup, took a good swallow and fell to her knees once more. This time several pairs of hands heaved her up and whisked her out the door to the right of the sanctuary.

They sat her down in a chair in the parish hall and asked if she needed an ambulance. "I'm fine," she said. "I'm wonderful." Still, they wouldn't allow her to return to the service but insisted she rest for a while.

Suanne had been too caught up in her sensation of rapture to notice the faces of those who had brought her there, but when all but one of them had returned to the nave, her eyes were able to focus on the woman who stayed behind. It was Maggie, who had been among the first people to welcome Suanne the first day she had attended. Maggie was several years older than Suanne and always wore a scarf to cover the wispy strands of hair that had grown in after her chemotherapy last year. They had had each other over to dinner on numerous occasions, and though they weren't perhaps the closest of friends, Suanne felt she could trust her.

"Has that ever happened to you?" Suanne asked.

Catching the awkward look on Maggie's face, Suanne hurried to explain. "I don't mean the falling down part, but the, the sense, that feeling, that—I hardly know how to explain it."

Maggie reached over and patted Suanne's knee. "Just rest a bit. I'm sure it will pass."

Suanne wanted to tell her she hoped it would never pass, but she sensed that perhaps Maggie really hadn't ever experienced anything like this. It seemed sad to her, at that moment, to think that Maggie might have gone through the pain and fear of cancer without the feeling Suanne had just been given that everything was going to be all right. That everything already was all right. She put her hand over Maggie's and smiled at her.

When the last hymn was sung and people started streaming in

for coffee hour, Suanne repeated a dozen times or more that it had been a dizzy spell but she was fine. She wondered if someone there would understand what she had experienced, but she couldn't find the courage to ask anyone else.

As she walked home, hoping to have some time in the attic before Bill returned from his golf outing, she was alarmed to notice the glow of her experience slowly fading. She quickened her pace, thinking that perhaps the feeling would return when she got back to Narnia.

Back in her attic, Suanne raced through *The Silver Chair.* So engrossed did she become in the story that she didn't hear the door open downstairs. Jill Pole was just slipping into the hole beneath the ruined city when she heard her husband call her name.

"Suanne?"

She jumped at the sound, realized he was at the foot of the ladder, and called out, "Here I am."

"What are you doing up here, sweetheart?" he said, climbing till his head poked up through the floor.

A list of possible excuses rushed through her mind, but in the end she lifted the book and told the simple truth. "Just reading."

Bill frowned and climbed up the rest of the way, ducking his head against the low slant of the roof. He scanned the attic with his usual expression of bemused concentration, then picked his way over the rafters and sat down beside her. "Whatcha reading?"

She showed him the cover. He put his hand on the book's spine and tilted his head back in order to see more clearly. "The Chronicles of Narnia," he read, and looked hard at his wife.

"Why'd you buy a new set? What's wrong with the one on the bookshelf downstairs?"

Suanne sat speechless. She didn't know what reaction she had expected, but it had never occurred to her that Bill might have read these books, let alone that he might own a set of them.

Bill put his arm around her shoulders and said, "I see you've got your ginger ale. Have you found the door into Uncle Andrew's study?"

Suanne leaned her head against Bill's shoulder. For some reason there were tears in her eyes. "Not yet," she said, "but I haven't looked very hard. I've been too busy reading."

"*The Silver Chair*," said Bill. "That's the one with Muddleglum, isn't it?"

"Puddleglum," she said.

"That's the one. I thought you never liked fantasy."

She considered for a moment. "These don't seem like fantasy. They seem—"

Bill nodded his head, as if he understood.

"Bill, do you believe Aslan is real?"

Bill erupted with a laugh that sounded like a bark. "Lewis pronounced it 'Ass-lan.' And yes. Yes, I suppose I do."

"How come you've never talked about him before?"

"I guess I thought you'd think I was being disrespectful of God."

Slowly, uncertainly, she said, "I think I met him today."

Bill looked at her face, leaning back as he had done when reading the book cover. "Are you feeling all right, Suanne?"

She smiled, but it was a somber smile. She thought of how the children had been both glad and solemn in Aslan's presence. "I don't know how to explain it. It was during Communion at church today. I just . . . I felt like he was standing in front of me, or as if I was suddenly standing in front of him. I just fell to my knees. I'm afraid I made something of a spectacle of myself."

"I can imagine," Bill said, gently.

"They rushed me right out of there, as if I'd just had a stroke. It would have been humiliating, but—it was wonderful."

Bill nodded again, gave her shoulders a squeeze and got awkwardly to his feet. "I don't want to keep you from Narnia. Keep reading," he said, "I'll make us some supper."

Suanne reached up and squeezed his hand. "Thank you," she said. While Bill climbed down the ladder, she took one moment to be amazed at his understanding before returning to Jill's flight from the giants' hounds. By the time the three adventurers had slid down the avalanche and the Undermen lit their lamps, the attic had receded and there was only the seemingly endless journey through Underworld.

She was stiff and sore when Jill and Eustace returned in triumph to Experiment House, and she found it difficult to start the journey down to the kitchen, whence came the aroma of Bill's signature tuna casserole. She wanted desperately to pick up the last book, but she forced herself to her feet and faced the ladder. "I wish," she said, but she couldn't finish the sentence. "What do I wish for?"

Over dinner, Bill talked about his golf game and retold a joke that his buddy Hank had told that made little sense to Suanne. After Bill had laughed at it all over again, he was quiet for a time. Then he spoke up.

"So did you, um—Aslan, when you met him, did he give you a quest?"

Suanne put down her fork and looked at him, searching his face for a sign he was making fun of her. He was staring at his food, and there was no trace of a smile on his lips.

"No," she said. "I don't think so. There were no words really, just a feeling of, of Presence."

"Mm," said Bill, shoveling another forkful of casserole into his mouth.

"I want him to, though. I hope he does."

"Hmp!" snorted Bill. "Be careful what you wish for."

Suanne said nothing. When she was finished eating, she thanked Bill for the meal, put her dishes in the sink and returned to the attic. Before she started *The Last Battle*, however, she offered up a simple prayer: "I do wish for it, though."

It was after midnight when she finished *The Last Battle*, and Suanne was troubled. When Tirian entered the stable and met Lucy and Peter, her heart had leapt at the prospect of meeting Susan again, but Tirian had asked after her, and Peter's reply had smitten Suanne's heart: "She is no longer a friend of Narnia." Then Lady Polly had gone on to describe Susan's downfall at the hand of vanity and worldliness, and Suanne had wept.

Now, at the end, she understood that Susan was not lost forever to Narnia but that her lack of faith had prevented her from being on the train when it crashed. The more Suanne thought about it, though, the more upset she became. If Susan had not been on the train, then she had lost her entire family in the crash. She tried to tell herself that Susan wasn't real, but it didn't help. Susan felt real. She would be Suanne's age by now. How had she managed? Suanne wished she could visit the woman somehow. It didn't seem fair.

A flash of anger startled Suanne, and she found herself flinging the book across the attic. "I hate you," she hissed between clenched teeth. "You and your Narnia can go to —"

"Everything all right up there?" called Bill.

"I'm fine, dear," said Suanne.

"Okay. I'm going to bed. Don't stay up too late now." She listened to his footsteps pass the ladder and enter the bedroom.

Suanne leaned back against the wall and slowly unclenched her fists.

After a time, she said softly, "I'm sorry."

On a sudden impulse, she got up and pulled the string that turned off the light. Carefully, she sat back down and waited. "If you're real," she murmured, "you'll speak to me." She gathered her knees beneath her chin and waited, trying to empty her mind of all thoughts that might get in the way of her hearing whatever voice might speak to her. She waited a long time, but the only voices she heard were ones that said no voice would come.

After a time her eyelids grew heavy, and she wanted nothing more than to crawl into bed next to Bill and forget the whole thing. She leaned forward, preparing to stand.

"Go for a walk."

Suanne blinked. Caught between standing and sitting, she tried to puzzle out whether the voice had been anything other than her own imagination. Sleep was all she wanted, but she had asked for God to speak to her. Could she then ignore him if he had? It might have been nothing more than a glitch in her imagination, but on the other hand, she was not in control of what God said to her, nor could she expect to understand the reason for what he might choose to say. In the end, being the practical person she was, she decided the only question worth asking was whether or not she was willing to go for a walk. She decided she was.

As she made her way down the ladder, she considered telling her husband where she was going, but he was already snoring steadily, and she had a sensation almost of being pulled down the stairway and out the door. She was at the sidewalk and taking a sharp left before it occurred to her that it wasn't safe for a woman of her age to be walking the streets so late at night.

The danger, though real, was quickly trumped by glory. The moon was full and so bright she could almost see colors. The air was warm, with only the slightest of breezes to lift smells to her nose. There was no sign of any other soul, and it amazed her to think that all this beauty should go unappreciated.

When the sidewalk emerged from under the trees for half a block, she had a good look at the moon, and for perhaps the first time in her life she really looked at it. It was smaller than she would have expected, and so bright that it seemed featureless until her eyes adjusted. The urgency she had been feeling up till this point, the sensation of being pulled, subsided. She wondered why God (if it was God) would want to bring her here particularly, and in such a hurry.

A flash of imagination caused her to laugh aloud. It was an image of a child grabbing her hand and pulling, desperate to show her some mundane thing that glowed numinous to ingenuous eyes. Dutifully she stared at the moon, wondering what on earth she was supposed to be seeing.

Quite suddenly she recalled a scene from *Prince Caspian*. After the battles were won and the feast was over, everyone else fell asleep, while Aslan and the Moon stared at each other with joy unblinking all night long.

She took a second look at the moon. The Lady of the Green Kirtle had asked what the sun (if it existed) could possibly be hanging from, and Suanne had to admit, it seemed improbable that the moon should hang motionless in the sky from nothing at all. Yet there it was, barely out of reach, reflecting the light of the sun most completely when it was the farthest away, able to lift oceans, connecting lovers half a world apart.

There were tears in her eyes as she lifted her hand to her heart. A swell of affection for the barren satellite rose up within her like a tide. For a moment she could imagine standing there all night reflecting on the different meanings of the moon. Unfortunately, the moment she imagined it she began to notice the crick in her neck, the ache in her calves and worst of all the picture of herself from a neighbor's point of view, standing outside in the middle of the night gaping at the moon.

With one last longing look at the moon, she turned to go inside. As soon as she started walking she became aware of how deeply tired she was. Yet when she reached her bed, though she climbed in without taking off her clothes, she didn't immediately fall asleep. Instead she found herself thinking about Ryan. If God himself had pulled her outside to look at the moon with the eagerness of a child, perhaps Ryan could continue the lesson, teaching her to see the world with new eyes. He had, after all, been the one to introduce her to Narnia. She resolved to spend more time with him, starting tomorrow. She drifted at length to sleep with visions of following him everywhere, overcome with wonder at each new ladybug and cloud.

She woke up from a dream both sad and wonderful that she couldn't quite remember except that she had been paddling a tiny boat toward an island in a wide blue sea. The lapping of the waves against her craft had been so soothing that she just wanted to lie there for awhile, submerged in the peace.

A sidelong glance at the clock told her it was almost nine o'clock. She hadn't slept so late in decades. A glance in the other direction told her that Bill was already gone. She pulled her feet out from under the sheets and reached for the phone on the nightstand to call Jeffrey's house before Ryan's day was planned out.

"Thanks for calling," said her son's sleepy voice. "I forgot to set my alarm again. It should have gone off twenty minutes ago. What's up?"

Suanne considered telling Jeffrey about her experience with

the Chronicles, perhaps apologize for discouraging him from fantasy when he was younger, but for some reason she felt shy. It was too new yet. "I wondered if I could spend some time with Ryan today," she said.

"Oh, sure, he'd love that. Diana got a call last night to go in and sub, so he was just going to daycare anyway. Can you be here in the next half hour?"

For a moment, Suanne felt the familiar resentment of being used by her son, but she decided this time to let it go. "Sure," she said, with barely a trace of ice in her voice.

She dressed quickly and made it to Jeffrey's condo within forty minutes. With an attempt at graciousness, she apologized for being late, but Jeffrey just said, "That's all right. I'm always late to work," and Suanne was helpless to stop her head from shaking in disapproval. Jeffrey smiled tightly and kissed her on the cheek. "Have fun, you guys. Don't wear Gran'ana out, Ryan." Ryan was playing with his trucks and didn't look up when his father left.

Suanne got down on her knees. "So what shall we do today?"

Ryan shrugged, intent on pushing a big yellow dump truck back and forth.

"Would you like to go to the zoo? See the lions?"

Ryan pushed a lever that lifted the dump truck's back end and blew a raspberry.

A shadow of worry passed over Suanne's mind. This was not how she had imagined the day would begin. Taking a deep breath, she said, "I know. Let's go to the park. We can play on the jungle gym and feed the geese."

At last Ryan looked up and held out his hand. Suanne took it, and after a brief detour to grab a box of cereal off the top of the refrigerator, they walked to the park.

The morning air was cool, the wind brisk and the sky crowded with white puffy clouds. Suanne and Ryan reached the park in ten or fifteen minutes. Ryan's small hand in hers made her feel, as they walked, like a queen, as though all that they passed was hers, though whether she was giving it all to Ryan or he to her she couldn't say.

They sat on a bench and opened the cereal box. Within a matter of minutes they were surrounded by Canadian geese. Ryan tossed tiny doughnut-shaped pieces of cereal to the geese with a serious, single-minded devotion.

Idly, Suanne tried to see the geese through Ryan's eyes, to find some wonder there, but all she could see were big ugly birds greedily jostling for position. Ryan seemed hardly to see them at all. Her hopes of the night before were dissipating. Perhaps the wide-eyed wonder of little children was nothing more than a fantasy grown-ups projected on them. Perhaps the real wide-eyed wonderers were first-time parents.

A couple of the geese were eyeing her, waiting for her contribution. She reached into the box and cast a handful of cereal bits before them. Briefly, as they gobbled up the pieces, her animosity toward them softened.

"Guess what, Ryan. I finished reading the Chronicles of Narnia last night."

"Hurray!" he said, throwing a handful of cereal straight up.

Suanne laughed. Ryan giggled and did it again.

"Hey, I know," he said, "we can play Narnia."

"How does one 'play Narnia'?"

"You be Aslan and I'll be the dragon, and you have to chase me."

Suanne tried not to show her disappointment. Chasing games were not her forte. Nevertheless she heard a voice in her head that may or may not have been Polly Plummer's: *I'm game if you are.* She put her hands up by her face and shaped them into claws. "Grr," she said. The growl sounded more old-womanish than leonine, and she was afraid Ryan would only laugh at her. Instead he squealed and bolted away, scattering geese in every direction.

Suanne stood up and shook her glorious mane. A rich wild aroma filled her nose, and she roared for joy before taking up the chase. 🌿

Reflection and Discussion Questions

THE LION, THE WITCH AND THE WARDROBE

1. How do Edmund's failings ultimately contribute to the Witch's demise?

2. Have you ever seen how God has used your own sin for his glory (Romans 8:28)? Tell the story briefly.

3. Meeting Aslan both affirms the children's identities and calls them to lose themselves. Where do you see this paradox in Scripture (perhaps in the words of Jesus or the life of David or Peter)?

   Where do you see it in your own life?

4. What dimensions of the cross are highlighted for you by Aslan's self-sacrifice?

5. "God is all about relinquishing power": do you agree? Why or why not?

6. Playing tig with Aslan and tending to the wounded are both appropriate responses to his victory. Do you tend to focus on intimacy with God more than service in the world, or vice versa?

   How is God calling you toward obedience and wholeness?

PRINCE CASPIAN

1. How is it that stories can be more powerful in convincing us of the truth—or of lies—than abstractly stated concepts? Give an example from your experience or observation.

2. Summarize Nikabrik's and Trumpkin's differing responses to the anti-Narnia forces.

3. Do you know of individuals or communities that have responded to hostility by "grabbing hold of [their] opponent's sword from the wrong end"?

   What was the result?

4. Why are the older Pevensies unable to see Aslan now?

   What qualities make Lucy able to see him?

5. What do Bacchus and his "wild girls" represent?

   Why do you think Lewis gives them a favorable role in *Prince Caspian?*

6. What invitation does Aslan offer the residents of Beruna?

   Do you need to hear and accept the same invitation?

7. In what ways have you tended to settle for hard work and routine rather than God's nourishment?

THE VOYAGE OF THE "DAWN TREADER"

1. What is it like to be a dragon—to be trapped in self-absorption, self-pity and disdain for others? Answer from your own experience if you can.

2. What great gifts does Eustace gain from his dragoning?

3. How do you respond to Reepicheep—and to human beings like him?

4. Is there such a thing as *noble* arrogance?

5. What temptations does the magician's book place before Lucy? Do you identify with her responses?

6. Why might our senses need to be strengthened—rather than diminished—for a close encounter with eternity?

7. What Gospel story is evoked by the image of a Lamb who has prepared breakfast on an open fire?

   Why do you think Aslan is a lamb here, rather than a lion?

THE SILVER CHAIR

1. Have you observed in society at large, or noted in yourself, a diminished propensity to help others when times are good or at least there is no crisis?

2. What problems of seeing and understanding bring Jill, Eustace and Puddleglum to the giant's castle?

   How do you relate this to St. Augustine's "I believe in order to understand"?

3. Describe the risks the three travelers face as they try to puzzle out how to respond to Prince Rilian's assurances and to discern the sign foretold by Aslan.

   How do they parallel our own struggles to hear and follow God's guidance?

4. Does the Queen's logic regarding the question of the sun's existence remind you of modern arguments against God's existence?

   Have you ever found such arguments compelling? Why or why not?

5. Like Rilian before the gnomic realm of Bism, how do we discern whether we should undertake an adventure that beckons us?

   How are the issues different depending on our temperament (whether we tend to be timid or foolhardy) and our circumstances?

6. What does it mean for our home to be a Person (Aslan/Christ) rather than a geographical place?

THE HORSE AND HIS BOY

1. Does the discussion of the initial "string of coincidences" remind you of unexpected divine appointments that have shaped your own life? If so, give an example.

2. When is giving up a moral failure, like Bree's failure to attempt to rescue his friends from the lion?

   When might it express the virtue of humility, a sober recognition that you are limited and creaturely?

3. Similarly, when does plunging into risk, like Shasta's leaping off Bree to confront the lion, reflect the virtue of courage?

   When might it express stubbornness or a sense of grandiosity?

4. Describe how Shasta, Aravis and the two horses respond as they stand before Aslan for a reckoning.

What dimensions of your own response to God's presence are pictured in them?

5. How do we assess the ultimate fairness of an outcome for ourselves or others?

6. Taking care to avoid pat answers, where do you see God's hand at work in redeeming your own suffering thus far? (Remember, your story is not yet over!)

THE MAGICIAN'S NEPHEW

1. Commercial messages in the media seek to persuade us to buy by suggesting that each of us *is* "the center of the universe." Give a few examples.

2. How is God's glorifying of us very different from such sales-driven manipulation?

3. Do you agree that evil is a negation of being? Think of examples to support your position.

4. What makes hopeful waiting a difficult process? Illustrate from the experience of Digory, Polly or the Queen, or from your own.

5. What is most moving to you in Lewis's portrayal of the creation of the universe?

   How does it deepen your worship of God as Creator?

6. How is humor, as well as justice (right relationships), a fruit of speech?

7. What strengthens Digory to resist the Witch's ultimate temp-

tation—her suggestion that he can save his mother's life if he bypasses Aslan's command?

How has closeness to God's heart strengthened your own resistance to evil?

THE LAST BATTLE

1. How do even the Narnians' good desires—their longing for Aslan's return—make them vulnerable to Shift's deception?

2. What false messiahs or false gospels in our own culture are particularly tempting for us? (Discerning this requires great objectivity and wisdom, but try to focus on what idols *you* find attractive rather than on the failings of others.)

3. In what ways has Puzzle's heart remained pure, though he has allowed himself to be used as a tool for deception?

4. How is Shift's name appropriate?

5. Do you recognize any Shift-y tendencies in yourself—to twist the true Story for your own benefit?

6. How might a Christian committed to pacifism nevertheless draw inspiration from the Chronicles' (and the Bible's) stories of bloody battle? (Those who are not pacifists should answer first, imagining empathically what an appropriate response might be, and then listen as the pacifists respond.)

How might these same stories encourage those who accept the just war position? (Reverse the order of response, seeking to maintain empathy.)

AFTERWORD

1. What do you think are valid criteria by which to evaluate the claims of world religions: their ethical teachings, their effects in society, their rootedness in history, or some other standard?

2. "We are called to lose": in what ways do you find this paradoxical assertion to be true for Christians?

3. How do "the most dangerous, difficult and desperate adventures" help us get to know God?

4. What are "Narnian eyes"?

   Have you, like Suanne, found yourself developing them?

5. Have you ever asked God to give you a quest?

   If so, what response did you receive?

Editions Used

CHRONICLES OF NARNIA

The Horse and His Boy. 1954. Reprint, New York: Collier Books, 1970.

The Last Battle. 1956. Reprint, New York: Collier Books, 1970.

The Lion, the Witch and the Wardrobe. 1950. Reprint, New York: Collier Books, 1970.

The Magician's Nephew. 1955. Reprint, New York: Collier Books, 1970.

Prince Caspian. 1951. Reprint, New York: Collier Books, 1970.

The Silver Chair. 1953. Reprint, New York: Collier Books, 1970.

The Voyage of the "Dawn Treader." 1952. Reprint, New York: Collier Books, 1970.

OTHER BOOKS BY C. S. LEWIS

Mere Christianity. 1943. Reprint, New York: Touchstone, 1980.

The Weight of Glory and Other Addresses. Revised and expanded edition. 1949. Reprint, New York: Macmillan, 1980.